INDUSTRY AND SOCIETY

Industry

AND

Society

Edited by

WILLIAM FOOTE WHYTE

Associate Professor of Sociology
The University of Chicago

FIRST EDITION
Sixth Impression

McGRAW-HILL BOOK COMPANY, INC.
New York and London
1946

THE COMMITTEE ON HUMAN RELATIONS
IN INDUSTRY

The Committee on Human Relations in Industry was organized at The University of Chicago in 1943 by W. Lloyd Warner, chairman, Burleigh B. Gardner, executive secretary, and Robert J. Havighurst.

The objective of the committee has been to carry on research in the social organization of industry and of our industrial society. This involves a study of the way in which factory and community mutually influence each other. We have also been investigating the problems of building cooperation within our industrial structure.

The research data have been gathered through field observation and interviewing. Some of our research assistants have held full-time or part-time jobs in industry in order to explore that world through experience and observation. These students have kept detailed work diaries, which record day by day the significant human events of the work situation. Other students have carried on research within the factory or in the community through interviews and observation.

Besides the research, members of the committee have carried on various related activities. We have discussed our research findings in courses taken by regular university students and by executives and personnel men and union officials. In the summer of 1945 we conducted a seminar on Human Relations in Industry in which all these groups were represented. This book grew out of our Human Relations in Industry lecture series held also in the summer of 1945.

The findings of our studies have been communicated to

executives in the sponsoring companies through numerous informal discussions and through periodic dinner meetings.

The research has led to publication of a number of articles, and with this volume we have launched a Human Relations in Industry Series. The second volume in the series will be *Human Problems of the Restaurant Industry* by William Foote Whyte. Other volumes presenting our research findings analyzed in terms of the approach of *Industry and Society* will appear from time to time.

The business organizations that have sponsored our research are Container Corporation of America, Goodman Manufacturing Company, Libby, McNeill and Libby, Link-Belt Ordnance Company, National Restaurant Association, The Radisson Hotel, Sears, Roebuck and Company, Soreng Manufacturing Company, Visking Corporation, and Western Shade Cloth Company.

The members of the Committee on Human Relations in Industry are W. Lloyd Warner, Departments of Anthropology and Sociology; George Brown, School of Business; Allison Davis, Department of Education; Burleigh B. Gardner, School of Business; Frederick Harbison, Department of Economics and executive secretary of the Industrial Relations Center; Robert J. Havighurst, Department of Education; Everett C. Hughes, Department of Sociology; Neil Jacoby, Vice-president of The University of Chicago; and William Foote Whyte, Department of Sociology.

WILLIAM FOOTE WHYTE.

CHICAGO, ILL.,
October, 1946.

CONTENTS

INDUSTRY AND SOCIETY

Chapter I

HUMAN RELATIONS IN INDUSTRY

TODAY we stand in one of the most crucial periods in the history of man. We have seen a steadily accelerating tempo of scientific and technological development. We have opened doors to knowledge so vast that no one can foresee the end and scientists themselves dread the powers that lie within their grasp. And this knowledge has been steadily converted into tools and ability for production, into skills and know-how, until we now have at our command the power to produce all that is needed to destroy hunger, want, and fear. We have the power to build a social order in which we all have opportunity to live and to make the most of our abilities and ambitions and in which none of us is condemned to a life of hunger, filth, and disease, a struggle merely to stay alive.

Although these powers are in our hands, we have not yet gained these goals. While technology moves ahead, a growing and irresistible tide of knowledge, our advance toward a happier life has lagged. Through the thirties we saw the tragedy of factories idle and food wasted while millions suffered want. And it was only through war, through production for sorrow and destruction, that we achieved full use of our productive powers.

It is clear that while we were building the machines of production we failed to develop the social organization that could use them to create a better world. With the rise of industrial society we see a decline in our ability to live and

1

work together in harmony. We see industries torn by strife with management and labor arrayed against each other. We see new groups—office workers, engineers, foremen—organizing to protect themselves. We see what should be well-integrated and cooperative units split into warring factions. We see all too clearly that, while management is able to organize machines and processes into well-integrated and efficient systems for production, it has much to learn about developing effective human organizations.

Yet in spite of the conflicts we see evidence that harmony and cooperation can be attained, both within industry and among nations. There is a growing mass of evidence that the goals can be achieved, and that an understanding of the processes of the society that will enable us to develop effective organizations can be reached.

As exploration of these problems proceeds it becomes increasingly clear that if we are to make an industrial society work, we must understand its human as well as its technical aspects. We must understand the world of the factory in which so many millions spend their lives. And we must understand just how that world reaches out into the large community. And from this we must develop the concepts and hypotheses, the ways of thinking, that will enable us to develop effective and cooperative organizations.

With these problems in mind we have organized at The University of Chicago the Committee on Human Relations in Industry. For over three years we have been studying fundamental problems of the social organization of industry and of our industrial society. With the cooperation of a number of companies and labor unions our research people have been able to observe and interview in a variety of situations. They have probed the details of the structure and the functioning of work groups. They have watched the processes of readjustment following changes in the system. They have examined the relationship of morale and cooper-

2

ation to the form of the organization. They have studied
the integration of workers in their families and neighborhoods and their patterns of general social adjustment.
From all this searching and probing we are gradually evolv-
ing a more adequate understanding of these problems and
a more useful set of concepts for exploring them.

To this research the committee brings a well-integrated
point of view and methodology. We see the society and any
of its segments, whether a neighborhood, a factory, or a work
group, as having a social structure comprised of the relations
among individuals. While there are obviously those individual differences which we call "personality," much of the
behavior whether in acts or talk or thinking is an expression
of the place of the individual in the social system rather than
an expression of his own unique personality pattern. The
primary interest in this research is directed to the understanding of the social structure and the way in which it controls and molds the individual. In order to study this we
rely almost completely on interviews and observation, which
means that the research people must actually go out into factories and homes. Thus the analysis and understanding
grow out of an intimate knowledge of the way the people
actually act, think, and feel.

Chapter II

THE FACTORY AS A SOCIAL SYSTEM

BURLEIGH B. GARDNER

WHEN we examine any factory or business enterprise, we see a social organization in miniature, a small segment of the total society, operating within the environment of the society, and often reflecting within itself the stresses and conflicts that exist in that larger world. As industrial and technological development progresses, we see frequent evidence of conflict and maladjustment within these social systems, often appearing in new and disturbing forms. For example, in the last few years we have seen the rising power of industrial unions, accompanied by bitter conflicts. At the same time we see groups that have been traditionally management-oriented turning to unionism. One of the most striking of these developments has been the growth of foremen's unions, which means that a group long accepted as part of management is saying, "We are not really part of management and must defend ourselves against it."

Now in order to understand these developments, it is necessary to understand the nature of the human organization and the stresses it imposes upon its members. In other words, let us examine the social structure the way an engineer would examine the structure of a machine in order to determine how it works and how the stresses affect the various parts.

In the first place, we see that in any concern there is an intricate pattern of relationships among people that links

4

them all together. Each has his place and function in this pattern and is so tied up with the whole that changes in any part of the organization may affect him and his job in often unexpected ways.

Within the whole there are certain patterns of relationships, certain types of structure, that are typical of industrial organizations. In examination of almost any organization there can be seen what we call the formal organization. This is what appears on any organization chart, and it is

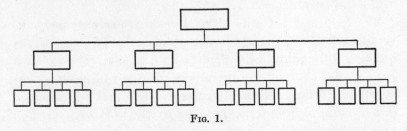

FIG. 1.

generally shown as a series of positions forming a fan-shaped pattern extending from the president or plant manager at the top to the workers at the bottom.

Here we find each position in the organization indicated, the functional division of duties, and who reports to whom. This is the pattern set by management; it is imposed from the top in accordance with the way management thinks the organization will function best. Much of this formal pattern follows lines of functional divisions in activities, and we see the separation of activities such as production, engineering, sales, accounting, etc.

This formal organization as shown on the charts is a system of positions that are occupied by people. The position defines the duties and functions of the individual in it; it places him in relation to others; it indicates whom he reports to and who reports to him. Along with the organization chart we sometimes find job descriptions that attempt to present a detailed statement of the duties, responsibilities, and authority of each position. And this further defines the place and activities of the person filling that position.

In addition, we find other patterns of relationships that do not appear on organization charts. We see little cliques of people who gather together for lunch or a game of cards at noon, or who meet together after work. We see friendships and antagonisms, people who identify with each other on one ground or another, groups who hold aloof from others, and a wide variety of activities that constitute what we call the "informal organization."

The informal patterns of relationships are extremely diversified and vary greatly in degree of stability. Sometimes a clique will maintain its identity and its interaction over a long period of time; in other cases groups will be in a constant state of flux. In many cases the informal organization develops out of interaction imposed by the work organization and by the formal organization. Friendships develop between people working side by side, cliques develop within work groups, or among people brought together through work contacts. Foremen or executives may form luncheon groups, or may golf or play cards together, or join the same social clubs. This also means that changes in formal structure usually result in changes in the informal organization; the promotion of an individual may throw him into new groups, or a general change in structure may set up new functional patterns of interaction and new patterns of informal relationships.

While formal organization and the contacts and interactions imposed by the work influence the informal organization, they do not determine it. In fact, it is a spontaneous development, which usually arises without the conscious or deliberate intent of those involved. Thus, as contrasted to the formal structure which can be imposed from above by decision of management and which can be readily presented in the form of a chart, informal organization develops from below and is often vague and difficult to see.

Now these informal relations are not merely a matter of friendly association and conversation unrelated to work behavior. Numerous studies have shown that they play a major role in determining the attitudes and behavior of workers with respect to their work, their superiors, and the company. In fact, the most powerful controls over the individual lie in the hands of the group itself and are expressed through the informal structure. Thus we see the work group deciding upon the proper standards of output and taking pains to see that the newcomer understands and conforms to these unofficial standards, which usually means restriction of output to the level the group finds satisfactory. Or we see the individual forced to choose between his superiors or the group. As one worker said, "You gotta decide whether to go along with the group or to stand in with the boss. And if you don't go along, the gang can make it mighty unpleasant."

Furthermore we frequently find that the standards set by the group are not in accord with those set by management. All too often the informal organization at the work level sets itself in opposition to the demands coming from above and works counter to the objectives set by management. As a result management feels that the informal organization is something that (1) it did not design and cannot control and (2) that is constantly interfering with the operation of the organization and standing in the way of management's plans. As a result one of the first questions executives usually raise when discussing informal organization is "How can it be done away with?" Unfortunately it is just one of the characteristics of human organizations; a characteristic that may be understood and modified but never done away with.

Another important characteristic of the factory organization is the presence of complicated sets of status systems. If we take the ordinary organization chart we see that the various positions are fitted into a series of ranks in which the president is superior to the vice-president, the plant manager is superior to the foreman, and the foreman is superior to the worker. Thus we have a series of status levels ranging from the large mass of workers at the bottom to the single individual at the top (see Fig. 2).

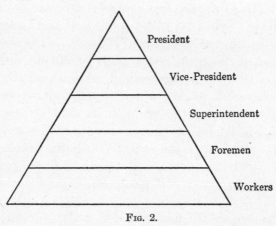

President

Vice-President

Superintendent

Foremen

Workers

Fig. 2.

In this system each person at one level outranks those in the levels below. He is somehow superior, his ideas carry more weight, and he is deferred to by those below. Each in turn gives deference to those above so that throughout the system we see people acting toward others in ways expressive of their relative positions. The extreme development of this can be seen in military organizations, where rank determines who salutes whom, who gives orders and who takes them, or who eats and associates with whom.

But this formal status system is only one of many that operate in the factory. We see also a sharp status distinction based on type of work, one of the most striking of which is the separation between office, or "white-collar," and shop jobs. Somehow the man who works with pencil and paper, who sits at a desk, is felt to be superior to the one who works with his hands at workbench or machine. And the importance of this distinction must not be underestimated. Again and again we see expressions of the feeling of the superiority of the office workers; we hear that shop workers are "dumb" and "uneducated," or that they are "loud and coarse." We see office workers avoiding contact with the shop, objecting to sharing locker and washrooms with shop workers, and rebelling against transfer to shop jobs. And we see shop workers criticizing the office workers for their attitudes yet at the same time preparing themselves or their children for office jobs.

In addition there is a sharp status difference between men and women in our society. The woman may be respected as the wife and mother in the home, but when she ventures into the man's world of industry she must take a back seat. In general, we find the women fitting into jobs which are labeled as "women's jobs," which are simpler, lighter, and lower paid than the "men's jobs." (Of course, the wartime labor shortages have broken down many such restrictions.) And always the men look down on both the women and the women's jobs; they feel themselves superior and it is a severe loss of status to be placed in a woman's job or to have a woman placed in theirs.

There are also status differences connected with pay. To a great extent money is felt to be a measure of worth and the more the individual earns the greater his prestige. Thus the man who is paid $1 an hour is somehow more important than the one who gets only 75 cents an hour. Furthermore, we see distinctions based on the way one is paid, the shop worker is on the "hourly pay roll," the office worker on the "weekly pay roll," and the executive on the "monthly pay roll." Thus, we find a very complex status system based on how much a man is paid and how he is paid; and we see Joe demanding a nickel raise so that he will be just as good as

Jim, or Jack bursting with pride because he is now on the monthly pay roll instead of the weekly.

In addition there are the status differences on the kind of work. The skilled worker outranks the unskilled, the grade *A* mechanic outranks the grade *B* mechanic, the machinist outranks his helper, and the helper outranks the janitor, and so on. Here we see innumerable shadings of rank, some very clear and some very subtle, but all of significance to the people in the situation.

Finally we see the prestige that accompanies age. The old-timer either in years or service with the company stands superior to the newcomer, to the young "punk" who doesn't know what the score is.

It is evident that the individual has a number of different status positions; he may be an old-timer in a low-status job, or a woman secretary may earn more than male clerks. Thus it is rare to find an organization that has complete uniformity in status positions, *i.e.*, where type of job, rate of pay, length of service, etc., all are closely correlated so that the oldest male employee has the top position, highest pay, etc. However, there is considerable feeling that there should be some such uniformity; there is a feeling that old-timers should earn more than newcomers or should have the higher jobs, that women should be paid less than men, that a rise in job status or in the supervisory hierarchy should be accompanied by an increase in pay.

In this social system of the factory we find a great deal of interest in knowing just where people fit, especially with regard to status. Those of higher rank wish to be distinguished from those below, and in this effort we see the development of status symbols of various sorts. We see status significance attached to furniture, "the larger the desk the bigger the shot"; a large office indicates more status than a small one, and a carpet outranks linoleum. In fact, almost anything can take on status meaning. As a result anyone

10

in an organization can readily tell where others fit in relation to himself. He can spot those whom he outranks. And any change that upsets these status symbols is apt to create serious problems of morale. To move a man to a smaller desk, to put the machinist on a helper's job, to fail to give the proper status symbols to the newly promoted, all give rise to serious disturbances.

Returning to our formal organization we see that one of the most important elements in the structure is the relation between each individual and his boss. These man-boss linkages form chains extending from the man at the top to each individual at the bottom and are the lines of authority along which the "big boss" exercises his control. It is down these lines that orders, directives and questions, and other communications from the top generally move, and back up these lines come information and answers.

Now this man-boss relationship has certain characteristics that are of great significance. In the first place, the subordinate looks to his superior for the direction of his activities, for authority to act, and for approval or disapproval. He expects his boss to tell him what his job is, to tell him what is expected in the way of performance, and to judge his performance. It is rarely possible for the subordinate to decide what his job is and to go ahead and do it without feeling the need for his superior to know what he is doing and to sanction it. Furthermore, the opportunities for advancement largely depend upon the relationship with the boss; he is the one who rewards and punishes; he determines who will get a chance at a better job, or a raise in pay, or other recognition.

As a result we find considerable anxiety concerning the relationship with the boss, to a surprising extent people at every level have their attention focused on their superior. They are constantly concerned with the questions of "How does he judge me? How am I doing? What does he want?"

11

They are alert to anticipate his wishes, to avoid his censure, and to gain his praise. They are often sensitive to his every mood and constantly seek for the inner meaning of every word and gesture. If he is glum and unresponsive, does it mean he is annoyed? If he questions an action, does it mean he disapproves?

This concern over the boss gives the effect of everyone's looking upward along the line of authority. Attention is directed toward those above rather than toward those below. Each is more alert to the actions, attitudes, and expectations of his superior than to those of his subordinates. Each lies awake worrying over how his superiors judge him but gives only passing thought to how his subordinates feel about him, and, therefore, each is apt to feel cut off from his superiors and to feel that the boss has little time or interest for him.

Furthermore, for those in supervisory and executive positions there is the problem of getting their organization, *i.e.*, their subordinates, to do a good job. Thus they feel that their own success is at the mercy of those below and that all too often they are being blamed for the failure of their subordinates. As a result they tend to be constantly critical, always finding fault with the ability and performance of their subordinates. The department head feels that he could really be a fine foreman and wishes his foreman would do the kind of job he wants done, and the superintendent feels the same way about the department head, and so on up the line.

Now this complex organism we call a "factory" requires a high degree of coordination between its various parts if it is to operate smoothly and effectively. And to a large extent proper coordination depends upon communication between individuals, between all levels, and between different segments. It is the rare department that can function effectively if it is isolated and out of touch with the rest of the organization.

Of extreme importance are the processes of communication vertically in the structure. To a large extent top management is the center of control and direction and it is constantly communicating downward through the structure. At the same time there is a constant flow of information upward to it. Now the line of authority provides one of the most important channels for this flow; down it, step by step are transmitted orders, often of a very general nature, which are assimilated at each level and translated into more specific orders to be applied to each organization. Thus what starts out at the top as a general directive ends up as a very specific order for individuals at the bottom. In the same way information, starting as a mass of specific details at the bottom, is condensed and organized at each level until it reaches the top as a simple set of figures or a report on the desk of the top executive.

Because of the nature of the man-boss relationships this movement up and down the line presents certain problems. In many cases concern over what the boss wants leads to over-reaction to his commands, or to misinterpretations of unimportant comments or requests. The big boss inquires about maintenance costs. The subordinate wonders if he thinks they are too high and the shop finds there is a sudden clamping down on all maintenance work.

This same concern also affects upward communication. The subordinate is always trying to anticipate what the boss wants to know. He is reluctant to pass up unpleasant news and quick to pass up good news. He is prone to gloss over and put a favorable slant on bad news or to find an alibi for what may look like his failures. He is constantly alert to his superior's moods, watching for the favorable time to present some request or to put forward some new idea.

Thus in the line we find a channel of communication that works by fits and starts, which is apt to modify or distort what passes through, and which may constitute a complete blockage. And as a result we find that the man at the top is apt to be quite well insulated from the bottom so that he has only a partial and highly interpreted picture of what goes on. And at the same time the ones below are aware of this insulation and feel helpless to break through.

This picture of the factory system is complicated enough even when viewed in static terms, but American industry does not stand still. There are always forces for change operating both outside and inside the factory system.

For one thing we see the gradual changes due to changes in personnel. New people come into the system, others leave it, all grow older and acquire new knowledge or skill, and informal relations gradually change. All this tends to promote gradual changes in the entire system. At the same time the external environment is changing. Technological advances make available new materials, processes, and products. Over-all changes in the economic system take place. There are new legal developments, and the adaptation of the system to meet these external forces results in internal changes.

There is the struggle of individuals and of organizations for recognition and development. We see the engineer seeking increased authority and freedom of action in his dealings with the shop foreman. We see the operating department resisting the attempts of personnel to take over the hiring of people. We see superintendents working to increase the size and importance of their organizations. We see the general tendency of any segment to expand. At the top we find management struggling to keep all these forces under control so that a proper balance is maintained.

These forces for change do not hold sway unopposed. Every change tends to be blocked or retarded by resistances it meets within the factory system. Anyone familiar with organization is aware of a characteristic that can best be described as a state of equilibrium. There is a tendency to resist change, to go on doing things the way they have always been done. In this the factory is like a living organism that seeks to maintain a state of equilibrium and rallies its forces to restore the original state when any disturbance arises. The organization reacts much like the human body in healing wounds and fighting infection. Thus we see individuals or groups acting to protect themselves from changes, to slow down the rate of change, or reduce its effects to a minimum. This characteristic may express itself in the reluctance of an individual to transfer to another department, in criticisms of a new machine, or in delays in trying new methods. In the status systems we see also a tendency toward an equilibrium in which each individual finds his place relative to the others and any disturbance of this relative position gives rise to disturbances.

Now there are certain types of change that always seem to meet resistance, and they can be roughly classified into three interdependent groups. First, we have those changes that threaten to lower the status or prestige of the group and of the individual. Thus we see concerted resistance to an attempt to move office workers to a low-status shop location. Such a move threatens their desire to be recognized as a superior group. They fear they will become identified with the lowly factory workers. Or we see resistance to the bringing of women or Negroes into skilled work; to be forced to accept these inferior beings as competent mechanics degrades the job.

Then we see the changes that reduce the authority and scope of action and decision. Thus giving the personnel department control over hiring and firing takes away some of the authority of the foreman and makes him feel reduced in importance. Or we see management rebelling against the organization of its workers lest the union interfere with its "right to run the business."

Finally, we see those changes that disrupt the habitual routines. A change in accounting procedures may meet with severe criticisms primarily because it is a change, and the group reacts negatively to it, seeing all its faults and distrusting its virtues. Thus we often find the attitude of "it's always been done this way," a clinging to the familiar and accustomed methods, and a reluctance to try the new.

As we watch these systems operate we see certain tendencies that are of special significance, and one of these is the tendency toward segmentation. With increasing size we find increasing specialization not only of individuals but also of organizations. There develop separate segments concerned with production, sales, engineering, accounting, personnel administration, or other activities, each having its own hierarchy and its own lines of authority. At the same time this splits the total structure into vertical segments that must all be integrated into a cooperative whole.

In order to perform their function many of these specialists must originate ideas or initiate actions that affect other segments. The engineer is expected to develop improved methods for the shop to use. The personnel department tries to introduce better methods of supervision or employment. The sales department is trying to get the type of product it can sell, and so on. Yet at the same time each organization tries to protect itself against the demands of the others. There is a tendency for each group to be self-centered and to struggle for its own ends.

In many cases this cleavage and conflict is so widespread that every organization seems pitted against all others. And the fight may be only organization against organization, or it may follow horizontal lines of cleavage until each level is defending itself against the others—workers against management, foremen against their superiors, white-collar workers against shop workers. Often in such concerns there is a feeling that the worst enemy is within the walls and the major effort is expended in the internal conflicts.

Of great importance also is the tendency toward authoritarianism. In the first place there are hierarchical systems in which the major seat of direction and authority is at the top. And we see the one at the top, the big boss, trying to shape and direct the organization to build the kind of organization he desires and to select the kind of people to be fitted into the organization. While there may be checks and limitations of various sorts, nevertheless he is the one who can most effectively impose his will upon the organization. And along with this we see strong feelings of identification. He feels possessive and thinks in terms of "my" company; its success is his success, and its failure is his failure.

As we go down the line we see minor seats of authority with each executive and supervisor imposing his judgment and his will upon the organization below him. We see each level confident of its ability to make better decisions than those below and often afraid to rely upon the judgment of subordinates.

In extreme cases we see this leading to the development of very autocratic organizations with each level exercising almost dictatorial powers over the ones below. In these organizations we often hear the idea that the good employee should be a "good soldier," and that whether he be an executive, foreman, or worker he should accept the decisions and commands of his superiors and carry them out without question or hesitation. And such a concept implies the infallibility of judgment of the superiors. It suggests that the big boss has completely adequate knowledge and can be trusted completely to do the right thing.

Of course, no organization is completely like this. Few subordinates have such blind confidence in their superiors, and few superiors have such supreme confidence in themselves. But the tendency toward this autocratic organization does exist and the more dictatorial the organization the more autocratic are its minor powers.

Now these systems have one general effect on their members. They force the individual to fit himself to the system and allow little room for adapting the system to the individual. And the more autocratic the system the more rigid the framework to which the member must adjust. Thus the systems operate to kill initiative, the rewards are apt to go to the one who "gives the boss what he wants," to the one who plays it safe and never sticks his neck out. In the more rigid systems the only use of initiative is to put subordinates in their place. The "guy" who gets pushed around from above becomes adept at pushing around those below.

Yet at the same time we hear continual complaints at all levels about the lack of initiative in those below. The president, who is noted for his autocratic use of his powers, the one whose subordinates dare not question his decisions and judgment, states to the papers that he cannot retire because he can find no one competent to fill his shoes, and he bemoans the lack of aggressiveness and initiative in the younger generation. Or the foreman who is constantly critical of everything his skilled workers may do complains that they will take no responsibility but turn to him on every minor detail. While they bemoan the decline of initiative, we see them creating the kind of social environment in which initiative withers and dies.

As these organizations grow larger and more complex, we find there is increasing pressure on the lower levels, greater and greater restriction upon their freedom of action and decision, and in many cases an accelerated rate of change. This has the effect of disturbing the equilibrium of relationships that existed when the systems were simpler and there was less distance between top and bottom. Out of this condition has developed increasing anxiety and tension, and a rapid growth of industrial unions has accompanied it.

Applying the concept of equilibrium we can say that as certain developments disturbed the former equilibrium of relationships, new types of structures and activities developed until a new equilibrium was attained. Thus, as the workers felt more and more at the mercy of a large and impersonal system, or of an increasingly autocratic and restrictive management, they coalesced to form a new group, the union. Through this they were able to initiate action back upon supervisors and management, to protect themselves against the tendency toward autocratic control at the top, or even to defend themselves against too rapid a rate of change.

Another good example of the development of new mechanisms to restore equilibrium is seen in the rise of unions among foremen. Here is a group long identified with management. Not only has top management thought of these first level supervisors as being representatives of management, the noncommissioned officers of industry, but also the foremen themselves tended to feel a part of management and to feel set apart from the workers.

In small organizations the foreman developed an equilibrium in his relationships both with workers and with management. He had freedom of interaction with top management and in many plants his superiors were men like himself who had worked their way up from the bottom.

With the increasing size of organizations, however, he has become more and more cut off from the top and in many firms his superiors are now engineers and technicians, often brought in from outside the organization. He often feels that the former channels for advancement are now blocked. Thus he feels more and more that he is only a small cog in a big machine and that he is not really a part of management but only a tool to be used as management sees fit.

Now he might have adjusted to this except for two things. One is the rate of change that constantly gives rise to new demands on him. The various specialists are constantly introducing new methods, setting new standards of performance, and limiting his freedom of action and decision.

Thus he can never get things in a groove so that he won't have to worry. He can never adjust to the situation and endure it in peace, but must always be making new efforts.

Finally he faces the growing strength of the unions. As they grow in power they in turn limit his freedom of action. He can no longer go his accustomed way, but must be cautious lest he offend his subordinates. And what is often the bitterest pill is the fact that through the union the workers can get a hearing when he who is part of management is ignored. Thus he is caught between the pressures from above and below.

As a result of all these factors the foreman's position becomes unbearable. He sees no way out except to organize in his own defense. Thus we see another structure developing that serves to relieve the pressures upon the supervisory group and enables it to act upon the rest of the system. Thus the system moves toward a new state of equilibrium and after a period of vibration a balance among the various forces may finally be attained.

As we apply this system of analysis to various work situations, we find that it is a powerful tool for the understanding of conflicts and a guide to corrective measures. If any case of friction or lack of cooperation, or any instance of successful operation, is looked on as an expression of individual personalities, it is impossible to predict behavior or to anticipate trouble except on the basis of detailed knowledge of every individual involved. However, by analyzing such phenomena in terms of the structure of relationships involved, it is possible to see conditions that will give rise to disturbances and even to predict the particular groups or even individuals who will be affected. Through following such an approach, it is possible to build a science of human relations.

Chapter III

THE FACTORY IN THE COMMUNITY

W. LLOYD WARNER AND J. O. LOW

THE American social system has been drastically changed by the development of our industrial institutions; on the other hand, our industrial organization has become what it is by virtue of being a part of the larger American social system. The two are interdependent and mutually influence each other, yet we know almost nothing about the nature of the relations that exist between the two. Much is known about the factory as a production and economic unit, but little is known about the influence of the factory on the community and the community on the factory. We shall attack the problem in the present chapter. To do so we shall concentrate our attention on one city where the factory and social system of the community were carefully studied over a period of years by a group of social anthropologists.

The relations of this factory and the community were studied when they were in equilibrium and the various parts of the factory and the city were well integrated and formed a functioning unit. They were also examined when industrial strife and social conflict had disrupted this equilibrium. Social anthropologists study periods of social disruption to gain deeper insight into what normally takes place in a social system because crisis periods reveal and dramatize the important and significant factors that often lie hidden during times of peace and quiet.

We are going to examine a strike in the shoe industry of an American community to learn what we can about the place of the factory in contemporary American life.[1]

In the worst year of the depression all the workers in all the factories of the principal industry of a New England community walked out. They struck at management with little or no warning; they struck with such impact that all the factories closed and no worker remained at his bench. Management had said they would never strike, for the workers of Yankee City were sensible, dependable, and, by a long peaceful history, had proved that they would always stay on the job. Union men outside the city agreed that Yankee City could not be organized and held that the local shoe workers were obstinate and "always stupid enough to play management's game." Many of the workers had told us that there would be no strike. Most of the townspeople, from the autocrats of Hill Street to the people on city welfare in the clam flats, said Yankee City workers would never strike. But they did—the foreigners and the Yankees of 10 generations—the men and the women, the very old and the very young, Jews and Gentiles, Catholics and Protestants, the whole heterogeneous mass of workers left their benches and in a few hours wiped out most of the basic productive system from which Yankee City earned its living. Not only did they strike and soundly defeat management, but they organized themselves, joined an industrial union, and became strong union members.

The industrial battle was fought between the owners of seven factories and 1,500 workers. Four of the factories,

[1] We cannot deal with the whole problem here because of the limitations of space. All aspects of the problem are treated in detail in Warner and Low, *The Social System of the Modern Factory*, Vol. IV, *Yankee City Series*, Yale University Press, New Haven. Most of the material in this chapter has been taken from that volume. It is to be published in 1946.

"the larger ones," employed the vast majority of the workers and accounted for most of the "34,000-dollar weekly pay roll." This industrial war lasted a month. It began on a bleak and snowy day in early March and lasted well into April. There were three clearly marked periods, each with different objectives and strategy and in each the industrial workers and the managers were dominated by different feelings.

In the first period, when management and the union fought desperately to gain control over the workers, the union was successful in organizing the workers and management was prevented from regaining control over them. The second period began when all the workers requested the union to represent them in the struggle with management and the union, secure with the workers organized behind them, began frontal attacks on management. During this time each continued its intense efforts to influence and dominate public opinion in Yankee City. The union also won this fight since the public identified the union with the workers and most of Yankee City sided with the shoe operators. The final phase, that of mediation and peace negotiations, began when a government labor board entered and started a series of negotiations that terminated the strike. Other efforts had been made from the beginning but none was successful.

The ultimate objective of each side, to which each fashioned its strategy was, of course, to make the other side capitulate and accept its demands; for management this meant the workers would return to their benches under approximately the same working conditions and wages as they had left; for the workers it meant that the management would agree to their demands and increase wages and improve working conditions; and for the union officials it meant that the union would maintain its control over the workers and keep them members of their organization, and management would be forced to deal directly with the union and not with the unorganized workers.

Each side organized itself and developed its strategies of offense and defense. The workers' defense tactics were centered around maintaining their unity and defeating management's offensive strategy of breaking up the workers' group and of destroying their morale. Accordingly, the workers used ritual and ceremonial procedures, where recognized symbols of solidarity, such as the flag, patriotic hymns, and the American Legion band played prominent parts. They achieved a defensive organization by means of meetings, speeches, entertainments, and the formation of a large number of committees that gave the mass of the workers opportunities to participate and to become and feel a part of a powerful and aggressive group. They took offensive action against management by making a series of demands for better wages and working conditions, by picketing, by making attacks against management in the newspaper, and by using the platform to influence public opinion. Management's defense was always to take the offense. The tactics tried included sending foremen to talk to the workers individually and thereby separating them from the group, spreading discouraging rumors, advertising in the paper, insisting on secret balloting by the workers when they voted on the issue of returning to work, and, above all, threatening to move their factories elsewhere should the workers continue with their demands and join the union. Of course, it must be remembered that each side, throughout the strike, was being deprived of its income, labor of its wages and management of its profits.

The strike occurred almost to the very year of the three hundredth anniversary of the founding of Yankee City and the beginning of the shoe industry. Shoemaking was always important there, but it was not until near the end of the nineteenth century that it achieved its place of supreme importance in the economy of the town. From the beginning, shipping, shipbuilding, fishing, and the other trades of the sea had dominated Yankee City's economic existence and set their mark on the community. When the New England shipping industries disappeared, Yankee City turned from the sea and sent its many drummers, salesmen, and manufactured goods westward to make the profits necessary for the establishment and continuance of its factory system. It was then that the textile manufacturers moved into the lead, but throughout the whole period shoemaking contributed significantly to the economic life of the city and, by the end of the century, had risen to a commanding place. Yankee City's shoe workers and owners throughout this time were known everywhere in the country for the excellence of their products.

Although the economy of the city went through revolutionary changes, the social superstructure that guided and maintained the lives of its citizens remained very much what it had been at the end of the War of 1812. The physical city stretches in a thin rectangle two miles inland along the bank of a large river from the harbor. Here, when the field study was made, lived 17,000 people. They were distributed from the river bottoms and clam flats back to the high ground on which Hill Street is located. The people of high status, some of them the descendants of those who made their fortunes in the sea trade, lived on this broad, elm-lined avenue. The people of lowest status, many of whom could trace their ancestry through long lines of fishermen to the city's founding, lived in Riverbrook on the clam flats. Between the two were the "Side-streeters" who, appropriately enough, occupied a middle-class status.[1]

[1] The status and social structure of Yankee City are described in Warner and Lunt, *The Social System of a Modern Community* and *The Status System of a Modern Community,* Vols. I and II, *Yankee City Series,* Yale University Press, New Haven, 1941, 1942.

The upper class of Hill Street was composed of two levels; the "Old Families" who could trace their aristocratic position through an ancestry of many generations, and the "New Families" who had but recently achieved high status. In the latter group were several families who "got their money out of shoes." The upper middle and lower middle classes were very much like such people wherever they are found in the United States or, for that matter, in all English-speaking countries. They were the conservatives, who, dominated by a "Protestant ethic," maintained, and often controlled, the moral order of the city. Below them was the upper lower class composed of the "poor but honest workmen" who ran the factories. At the bottom were the "broken-down Yankees," often called the "Riverbrookers," who also worked in the factories and who did a moderate amount of clamming and fishing for a living.

Scattered throughout the status system from the lower upper class ("New Family" level) to the lower lower class ("Riverbrookers") were the descendants of the Irish and, at somewhat lower levels, the French-Canadians, Jews, Poles, Greeks, and other ethnic groups, who began settling in Yankee City in the 1840's and continued until 1924. They had their own social system that preserved an increasingly small stock of the ancestral culture while relating their populations to the larger world of Yankee City. The Yankees were dominant and the most powerful group in the city, but the ethnics each year increased their power and prestige while they shed their variant mores and accepted those of the dominant Yankees.[1]

All these people were involved in the strike; the bread of most of them was directly or indirectly earned in the shoe

[1] The social systems of eight ethnic groups are analyzed and the processes of assimilation described in Warner and Srole, *The Social System of American Ethnic Groups,* Vol. III, *Yankee City Series,* Yale University Press, New Haven, 1945.

factories. Men everywhere in the city asked themselves, when the strike occurred, why such a thing should have happened to the people of Yankee City. Each man had his own answer. The answer of each tended to reveal more about the life and status of the man who talked than about the cause or causes of the strike. More often than not the explanations were economic. These townspeople forgot that there had been serious depressions before and that there had been no strikes. Each of them forgot that there had been low wages before and that there had been no unions. Each forgot, too, that there had been strikes when wages were high and times were said to be good. Although these economic arguments supplied important and necessary reasons for the strike and the unionization of the workers, they were insufficient explanations.

It seems to us the secrets of industrial strife in Yankee City and elsewhere lie beyond the words and deeds of the strike. They can only be found in the whole life of the community in which the workers and owners are but a part. The answers of the economic determinists or of the historians, while important, are not sufficient.

If social science is to be of any worth to us, it must be capable of adding significance and meaning to human behavior that will give us deeper insight into human life and explain more fully than common-sense knowledge why human beings act the way they do. Science necessarily solves problems. To solve them it must know what questions need to be answered. Let us reexamine the questions implied in the statements of the Yankee City townsmen in a more explicit and pointed manner to determine if we can learn what happened in this industrial crisis and to see if such knowledge about the strike can tell us about other similar crises in American life.

The immediate questions are basic to the whole problem, but, of even greater importance, they lead us into more fundamental ones about the nature of our industrial society. We will endeavor to give at least partial answers to some of these larger questions.

The first questions we must answer about the strike are

1. In a community where there had been very few strikes and *no* successful ones, why did the workers in *all* the factories of the largest industry of the community strike, win all their demands and, after a severe struggle, soundly defeat management?

2. In a community where unions had previously tried and failed to gain even a foothold and where there had never been a union, why was a union successful in separating the workers from management?

3. Why was the union successful in organizing *all* the workers in *all* the shoe factories in the community?

4. Why was the union successful in maintaining the organization despite the intense and prolonged efforts of management to prevent unionization and break up the shoe union?

5. Why did Yankee City change from a nonunion to a union town?

Perhaps the best way to gain an understanding of the strike and of the relations of the contemporary factory and the community is to view the present in the light of the past. The history of Yankee City's shoe factories may be conveniently divided into four periods ranging from the earliest times when the family was the productive unit through the periods of early and late small-city capitalism to the present stage when mass production and the machine dominate the industry, and control has shifted to New York. Included were revolutionary technological developments, increases in the division of labor, radical modifications of ownership and control, and rearrangements of the relations of producer and consumer and of workers among themselves.

During the technological development of Yankee City's

shoe industry, the tools changed from a few basic ones, entirely hand-used, to machines in an assembly line; and their product changed from a single pair of shoes to tens of thousands in mass production. In the beginning, the family made its own shoes or a highly skilled artisan, the cobbler, made shoes for the family. In time, several families divided the highly skilled jobs among themselves and their families. Ultimately, a central factory developed and the jobs were divided into a large number of systematized low-skilled jobs. The history of ownership and control is correlated with the changes in the division of labor. In early days, tools, skills, and materials were possessed by the family. Eventually the materials were supplied by the owner manager and soon he also owned the tools and machines. The sequence of development of producer-consumer relations tells a similar pointed story. The family produced and consumed its shoes all within the circle of its simple unit. Then, the local community was the consumer-producer unit, and ultimately the market became national and even world-wide. Workers' relations changed from those of kinship and family ties to those of occupation, where apprenticeships and craftsmanship relations were superseded, and the industrial union became dominant in organizing the affairs of the workers. The structure of economic relations changed from the immediate family into a local hierarchy, and the locally owned factory changed into a vast, complex system owned, managed, and dominated by New York City.

With these several histories in mind, let us ask ourselves what would have happened if the strike had taken place in each of the several periods. In period one, with a family consuming and producing economy, such a conflict would have been impossible. The social system had not evolved to sufficient complexity; the forces had not been born that were to oppose each other in civil strife. In the second phase, several families in a neighborhood might have quarreled but it is only in one's imagination that one could conceive of civil strife among the shoemakers.

In the third phase, however, there appears a new social personality, and an older one begins to take on a new form and assume a new place in the community. The capitalist is born and during the following periods he develops into full maturity. Meanwhile the worker loses control and management of his time and skills and becomes a subordinate in a hierarchy. There are, thus, distinct and opposing forces set up in the shoemaking system. What is good for one is not necessarily good for the other, but the interdependence of the two opposing groups is still very intimate, powerful, and highly necessary. The tools, the skills, and the places of manufacture belong to the worker, but the materials, the place of assembly, and the market are now possessed by the manager. Striking is possible but extremely difficult and unlikely.

In the fourth period, full capitalism has been achieved; the manufacturer is now the owner of the tools, the machines, and the industrial plant; he controls the market. The workers have become sufficiently self-conscious and antagonistic to machines to organize into craft unions. Industrial warfare still might prove difficult to start, although it did occur, because in a small city where most people know each other, the owner and manager more often than not knows "his help" and they know him. The close relation between the two often implies greater compatibility and understanding that cut down the likelihood of conflict. But when strikes do occur, the resulting civil strife is likely to be bitter because it is in the confines of the community.

In the last period, the capitalist has become the super-capitalist and the workers have forgotten their pride in their separate jobs, have dismissed the small differences among them, and have united in one industrial union with tens and hundreds of thousands of workers throughout the country combining their strength to assert their interests against management. In such a social setting strikes are inevitable and certain.[1]

An examination of the status of the worker in the factory and in the community reveals another important factor contributing to industrial strife. During the early periods of the factory in Yankee City a skill hierarchy dominated the

CHART I.

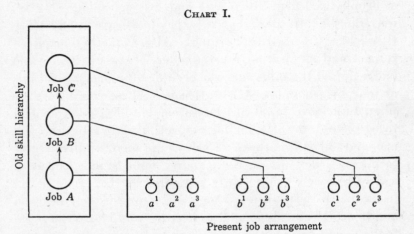

Present job arrangement

lives of the workers and helped establish their place in the community. The introduction of the machine into all parts of the production processes of the factory largely destroyed the skill hierarchy.

Chart I illustrates what has happened to craft and skill in the modern factory. The vertical hierarchy of skilled jobs has become a horizontal layer of low-skilled ones. Each of the skilled jobs has been divided into a number of simple, low-skilled ones and machines are performing most of the actions necessary for each job. Jobs formerly at the top and bottom of the hierarchy that were separated by higher and lower prestige and paid accordingly are now in the same

[1] See Chap. II of Vol. IV of the *Yankee City Series* for the details of this whole industrial development.

category of prestige and pay. We believe that the breakup of the skill hierarchy contributed importantly to the outbreak of the strike, to the course it took, and, in particular, to the coming of the union. The hierarchy of crafts that once organized the relations of the workers and provided a way of life for the shoe workers was really an age-grade system. Youngsters served their hard apprenticeship and, as neophytes, learned their task and, even more importantly, were taught to respect the skills they had learned and those they looked forward to learning. Above all, they acquired respect and admiration for the older men above them who had acquired the skills and who occupied the proud positions of journeymen and master craftsmen. These youngsters aspired to achieve for themselves a similar high position and to be the objects of a similar respect of their fellow craftsmen and fellow townsmen. Each young man, in direct face-to-face interaction with those above, imitated and learned a way of life while being highly motivated by the strong desire to escape the irksome limitations of his present low position and to attain the higher place where he would have the satisfaction of making his own decisions and possess the prestige and pay consequent to such great eminence. By the time he had learned how to do the things needed to equip himself for advancement, enough time had passed to mature him sufficiently to act the part of a man. There can be little doubt that age factors as well as those of skill determined the time for advancement. During this preliminary period he learned that he was a craftsman and that he had a particular place in the whole system, with responsibilities and obligations that, once acquired, gave him rights and privileges. Thus, while he internalized this behavior and all its values and their many subtleties and learned what he was as a man, he became an inextricable member of the honorable fraternity of those who made, and who knew how to make, shoes. In this system, workers and managers were indissolubly interwoven into a common enterprise with a common set of values. In this system the internal personal structure of each was made up of very much the same apparatus and their personalities were reinforced by the social system of shoemaking.

In learning to respect the skill of the master craftsman, the apprentice learned to respect himself. He had security in his job, but he had even greater personal security because he had learned how to respect it. And because he was a member of an age-graded male fraternity made up of other men like himself who had the knowledge and necessary skills to make shoes, he possessed that feeling of freedom and independence and of being autonomous that comes from leading a disciplined life. He spent his life acquiring virtue, prestige, and respect, learning as he aged and climbed upward and at the same time teaching those who were younger than he and who aspired to be like him.

Slowly this way of life degenerated and the machine took the virtue and respect from the workers, and at the same time broke the skill hierarchy that dominated their occupation. There was no longer a period for young men to learn to respect those in the age grade above them and in so doing to become self-respecting workers. The "ladder to the stars" was gone and with it much of the fabric of the "American dream."

When the age-grade structure that organized the male aborigines of Melanesia and North America into a hierarchy of prestige and achievement was broken under the impact of white civilization in many of these societies, the frustrations suffered by those who had once known self-respect crystallized into aggressive movements or into attempts to abolish the new ways and to retreat into the old and cherished ways of the past. There are, thus, some resemblances to developments in non-European societies.

The parallel between Yankee City's age-grade structure and theirs cannot be pushed too far but certainly the two share obvious characteristics. In the earlier days of the machine, the Knights of St. Crispin organized themselves and attempted to stop the further introduction of machinery, and most of them longed for the good old days when there were no machines, when a trained hand and eye did the job. These attempts failed and their organization collapsed, for they were not adaptive and could not stop the inevitable advance of our industrial technology.

When the whole age-grade structure of craftsmanship had almost entirely collapsed and the American shoe worker was thereby denied his share of the American dream, he and his kind were ready for any mass movement that would strike at those whom they charged, in their own minds, with responsibility for their unhappy condition. Much of this behavior was not conscious. Much of it was feeling rather than thought, as indeed were the feelings and thoughts that composed the mass movements of the aboriginal Melanesians and North American Indians. It seems certain, however, that American workers, taught from childhood that those who work and apply themselves and practice the ethics of the middle class would be rewarded by achievement and success, would rebel and strike back out of sheer frustration when they found out that the American dream no longer was true and that the hard facts belied the beautiful words they had been taught. It seems even more likely that the effects of the break in the skill hierarchy were potent forces that contributed their full share to the workers' striking and accepting the union as their champion.

Two other important causes of the strike must now be dealt with. The first is the expansion of the hierarchy upward, out of Yankee City, through the expansion of individual enterprises and the establishment by them of central offices in distant large cities. The second is the expansion of the structure outward from Yankee City through the growth of manufacturers' associations and labor unions, also with headquarters outside Yankee City and with units in many other shoemaking communities in New England and elsewhere. Both of these developments have gone on concurrently, each reacting upon the other. And both decrease Yankee City's control over its shoe factories by subjecting the factories, or segments of them, to more and more control exerted from outside Yankee City.

In the early days of the shoe industry, the owners and managerial staffs of the factories, as well as the operatives, were residents of Yankee City; there was no extension of the factory social structures outside the local community. The factories were then entirely under the control of the community; not only the formal control of city ordinances and laws, but also the more pervasive informal controls of community traditions and attitudes. There were feelings of neighborliness and friendship between manager and worker and of mutual responsibilities to each other and to the community that went beyond the formal employer-employee agreement.

In the days of local capitalism, the shoe manufacturers were accepted by all social strata as leaders of the total community. Shortly after the death of the most powerful of these business leaders, a number of prominent Yankee City men published a memorial volume that contained the usual words of high praise for great men. Since these same words, unlike those of many memorial volumes, were said about him by ordinary men of the street and were used during the strike, it is important to examine them. A member of one of the oldest families of Yankee City wrote:

He (the manufacturer) was one of the most remarkable men ever connected with Yankee City; a businessman of liberal culture, of fine literary taste, gifted as an orator, in music and theatricals. . . . He was an acquisition to any society. He honored any public station, however high. . . . He achieved

more in his fifty years of life than most men can point to after
marking a very old age. . . .

He was identified with the public health of this city and was
a conspicuous figure in all its great social functions as long as
his health permitted it. He was a leading financier and a man
who at once took and ever afterwards occupied a prominent
position in this community. For years, by common consent, he
was the leading man of the city. . . . Forcefulness of character made him the commanding spirit in every undertaking in
which he shared and in every circle in which he moved.

Our analysis of the manufacturer's participation in the
community provides the crucial evidence to show why he
became the powerful collective symbol that was used against
the contemporary managers during the strike.

In the business and financial sphere he was

1. Owner and head of his million-dollar shoe company.

2. President of one of the most powerful banks in the city.

3. Member of the Board of Trustees of the Financial Institute, a firm of the utmost prestige and power in the community.

4. Director of the Security Trust Company, another
powerful financial institution.

5. Director of the Yankee City Gas and Electric Company.

He was involved in a large number of civic enterprises and
was a member of many civic institutions. He was

6. Director and one of the founders of the city's most
important hospital.

7. Director of the Public Library.

8. Member of the school committee.

9. Trustee of the Revere Free School.

10. President of the City Improvement Society.

He also took an important part in politics. He was

11. Chairman of the Republican City Committee.

12. Member of the City Council.

13. Delegate to the National Republican Convention.
14. Mayor of the city.

He was also prominent in church and religious affairs. He was

15. President of the Yankee County Unitarian Club.
16. President of the Yankee County Unitarian Conference.

He was a leader in fraternal affairs and was

17. Past Master of St. John's Lodge.
18. Member of several important fraternal orders.

He was an active member of some of the most exclusive clubs of the city including

19. The Drama Club.
20. The Thursday Night Club.
21. The Friday Evening Club.
22. The February Club.
23. The Revere Club.
24. The Country Club.

The evidence demonstrates that in all these organizations he was active and powerful. This brief survey of some of his participation in the community demonstrates that his activities ramified throughout the city and that much of the life of the city was centered in him. It also demonstrates that he accepted responsibility for the larger affairs of the community and helped integrate its activities, for he provided responsible leadership for the whole life of the community. "He was a man you could depend on."

Very much the same could be said about his two successors. They, too, were responsible elders of the city. They not only provided jobs and wages through their factories, but they were citizens of the town and men who felt obligated to it. Their membership in local institutions compares very favorably with that of their predecessor.

In the days before big-city capitalism took control, the local enterpriser was financed by Yankee City banks. These banks and other investment houses possessed more autonomy and prestige then than they do now. In the development of the local shoe industry, local financiers played important and necessary roles and, at least part of the time, were silent partners in the business. Much of the wealth they derived from their investments was reinvested in Yankee City. The money was put into new enterprises, their own living, or civic activities. Their white Georgian houses on Hill Street, whose gardens bordered those of the manufacturers, were majestic symbols of their power and prestige and forever reminded and often reassured everyone of the visible presence of these powerful and protecting men in Yankee City.

The Yankee City financiers, too, were men of responsibility, dominated by sentiments of local pride. They did well for themselves, but they also did well for the city. Perhaps the price was high, but the product bought by the rest of the community was substantial and of high quality. Their philanthropies, combined with their power and leadership, contributed enormously to the city's development and provided a firm foundation for the larger civic life of the community. Parks, libraries, hospitals, societies to help the unfortunate and aged, foundations to send young men to college, endowments of schools, churches, and many other worthy civic enterprises were granted and maintained by the money and leadership of the local financiers and manager owners.

The essential point to remember for these leaders of industry and finance is that they were subject to local control (1) because they were dominated by local sentiments which motivated them "to take care of their own people," and (2) they were under the powerful influence of the numerous organizations to which they belonged and of their personal contacts with local citizens, which directly related them to influence from every part of the city.

The advent of big-city capitalism shattered this closely woven network of personal relations, loyalties, and obligations. Yankee City shoe factories are no longer owned exclusively by local citizens. More and more of them have been absorbed by larger enterprises whose executive offices are in New York City. At the time of our study, the largest shoe factory in Yankee City was owned by a company which operated several other factories in New England and which also owned the nationwide *ABC* chain of retail shoe stores, all of which were controlled from a central office in New York. Even some of the smaller Yankee City shoe factories, although still locally owned and managed, sold most of their shoes to chain-store organizations.

Yankee City has become but a pin point upon the map of industrial empire for these large investment houses. The flow of wealth from Yankee City's banks and factories, once a great local arterial system giving life and strength to the town, now has shrunk to an infinitesimal part of big-city, world-wide capitalism and is of no vital significance in the life of this great system.

The extent of this change may be seen from the following account of the finances of the *ABC* company, which appeared in a June, 1945, issue of a large New York newspaper:

A group headed by Oppenheimer and Co. and Brandeis and Son, and including the Stultz Co., has concluded an agreement for purchase of the majority of Lion Shoe Corp. stock, it was announced today.

Lion Shoe will be merged into its wholly owned retail subsidiary, the *ABC* Shoe Corp., with subsequent public issue of securities of the latter company.

Abraham Cohen, associated with the companies in an executive capacity for more than 20 years, will be elected president and general manager. Frederick Stultz, president of the Stultz Co., will be made chairman of the board.

The *ABC* Shoe Corp. owns a number of factories equipped to manufacture 20,000 pairs of shoes daily and operates a chain of 110 stores in 56 cities.

Decisions on these high levels of national and international finance are being made without regard for the needs and vital interests of Yankee City. The old ties between top management and the community have completely broken down.

As the vertical hierarchy of the factory system extended to executive offices in New York, even the local factory managers came to be, for the most part, "outsiders" and members of ethnic minorities. They had their factories in the town and some of them drove down to work in the morning and left at night. The workers knew or felt that the forces that controlled local men would not control these outsiders. The vast network of relations and memberships that made the former owners local leaders, as well as local manufacturers, had been reduced to a purely economic one of employer and employee. It was that and nothing more. It is small wonder that the workers during this strike "gave the horse laugh to the managers when they talked about being good fellows."

At the time of the strike the few local men who were managers, although born and reared in Yankee City, were little more than the factory managers for big-city capitalists, for they occupied inferior positions in this vastly extended vertical structure. They were not in a position to take leadership. They were not in a position of great power where they were free to make the decisions that always characterized the lives of the owners of the previous period.

Each of these local men felt what had happened very deeply and some of them were explicit enough about it to say so. We knew some of them well. They were not the weak or unscrupulous men that their opponents made them

40

out to be. Personally, they were men of good reputations in the business world. Some of them had been trained by their own fathers to be community leaders but their place in the new socioeconomic structure of Yankee City prevented them from playing this role and each in his own way contributed directly to the defeat of the managerial group. Part of their ineptness was due to their inability to measure up in their own minds to the great men of the past. This was a dead past, glorious and safe, when men knew themselves to be free men and Yankee City was "the hub of the universe." This whole period was symbolized in the memories of the workers and management by the names and reputations of the former owners. The lives of these men epitomized the period for all those who remembered. They symbolized the longing of everyone to return to those days when it was possible for one of them, with all his power and prestige, to stop and gently chide Sam Taylor, the cutter, for not calling him by his first name, and he and Sam could talk about "the trouble in the cutting room." Power was under control and security was present then; manager and worker were part of a self-contained system in which each knew his part in the total system.

In these days of big-city capitalism, when Yankee City had lost control of its own destinies, few workers would go up to the "big boss" to tell him "what's wrong in the cutting room," and those who did were not considered the respected friends of the workers but "stool pigeons who were getting theirs from management."

During the strike the local men cut poor figures as fighters for management's side. Two of them openly lined up with the strikers. Local sentiment and the feeling against "the foreigners" was too much for them. They materially contributed to the workers' victory.

One of them damaged the cause of management when he tried to fight the head of the union during a peace conference. Everyone said he blustered and acted badly when he used such tactics. He was under the control of higher management and occupied an inferior managerial position where he had little freedom to assume command and take leadership. Yet he had learned from "one of the grand old men" of the last period, when he worked for him, how his kind of man should act and he knew that an owner and manager should assume control. It seems a reasonable hypothesis that the conflict between his beliefs on how a manager should act and what he was permitted to do by his status greatly contributed to causing his unfortunate act, an act which materially aided the union. He tried to take command in a situation where it was impossible to do so, and instead of commanding he could only "bluster."

His antagonist, on the other hand, was "top manager" of the union. He did have power and he could make decisions. His beliefs about what should be done and his status were commensurate and he used them to the greatest effect for the cause of the union.

All these local men knew somehow they were not the men their "fathers" were and these dead men, symbolizing the glorious past, overawed and helped defeat them. While the men of yesterday are dead, "their souls go marching on" in the memories of the living. They have become collective symbols of that lost age when the prestige and power of local financiers and local producers "took care of our own people." These symbols were powerful influences upon the sentiments of workers as well as managers during the strike crisis. Sapping the confidence of the local managers, they gave strength to the strikers who dramatized their cause in terms of a struggle of Yankee City against big-city capitalism.

From this analysis of today's and yesterday's owners several important propositions can be offered that contribute to our understanding of the strike. The vertical extension of

42

the corporate structure of the shoe manufacturing enterprises had pushed the top of the hierarchy into the great metropolises and, in so doing, had brought in outsiders who were foreigners in culture, had no local prestige, and were lacking in understanding and feeling for the local workers and the town itself. This extension of the industrial hierarchy reduced the local men to inferior positions in the hierarchy, where they were incapable of making decisions and could not initiate actions that would give them the power of leadership for the workers and for the rest of the town.

The local managers, reduced to inferior statuses in the industrial hierarchy also occupied lower social class ranking in the community than their predecessors. This greatly reduced their strength as leaders who could form community opinion in times of crisis when the position of management was threatened. They could no longer lead the worker or the community. Because of this inferior position of the managers, those men in the community who would once have been their natural allies and who enjoyed top social class position were now above them and shared none of their interests, were hostile to them and friendly to the workers.

In "the good old days," the people of Yankee City felt that they all shared in a common way of life, in which business and industry was closely integrated into the community. This way of life had its frictions and conflicts, but it provided all the people with a set of common symbols to guide their behavior, and it also provided effective leadership from the top of the social order. Furthermore, these personal ties made it possible for workers to redress their grievances through going right up to members of management.

When New York financiers assumed control of the industrial hierarchy, the social and civic leaders of Yankee City were no longer active in local management. The management of industry was no longer directly tied in with the wider life of the community. This split between management and the community made it possible to mobilize the workers into an organization to fight management.

In the same period, the solidarity of the workers was strengthened by the breakup of the old skill hierarchy. No longer could the workers start at the bottom as apprentices and progress upward step by step as they grew older and acquired the skills and learned the way of life of the skilled craftsman. This age-graded skill hierarchy served to differentiate the workers from one another and to provide increasing security, prestige, and freedom with every step up from the bottom of the ladder. Now the rewards and satisfactions of this way of life are gone forever. Mechanization of the shoe industry has leveled the skills so that there is little room for such differentiation. When workers become interchangeable cogs in a machine, they come to feel that the only security for the individual lies in belonging to an organization of fellow workers.

What happened in Yankee City appears to have been happening throughout the country. With advances in technology and the development of big-city capitalism, the social distance between workers and management has been increasing, and we seem to be witnessing the emergence of an industrial working class.

The status of the worker has steadily deteriorated, and he has lost his chance to work his way up the craft ladder onto higher rungs of skill or into management. He has also lost the personal ties with management that might enable him to settle his grievances on an individual basis. Since the workers are now sufficiently alike to have had common experiences and anxieties, it is no longer difficult for the industrial union to organize them into a group for collective bargaining. Besides exerting economic pressure, the union gives the workers a new sense of strength and becomes a powerful weapon to force management to recognize their worth as men. To compensate for their loss of status and for their anxieties in a changing industrial civilization, workers have been trying to find status and security in union organization.

American industry has been undergoing far-reaching changes in technology and human relations. It is only through an understanding of the nature of these changes in our way of life that it is possible to explain the labor strife that spreads through the cities and towns of America.

Chapter IV

FUNCTIONS AND PATHOLOGY OF STATUS SYSTEMS IN FORMAL ORGANIZATIONS

CHESTER I. BARNARD

President, The New Jersey Bell Telephone Company

THE following is a report of a preliminary inquiry into the nature and functions of systems of status in formal organizations. So far as I am aware, this subject has not been given extensive consideration by students of organization. This neglect appears not to be due to failure to recognize the importance of problems of status in organizations but rather to failure to recognize that status is systematic and that systems of status have a considerable degree of independence of other structural aspects of organization. Status systems are very closely related, for example, to systems of specialization, to systems of organization communication, and to systems of authority, so that differences of status have appeared to be incidental to these other structural aspects of organization and not to constitute a separate system. This view appears to be inadequate.

Formal organizations are not independent societies but are rather limited forms of social behavior growing out of the more general societies of which they are part. This observation is especially pertinent to systems of status, particularly as respects their function of providing incentives, which largely depends upon the general conception of status obtaining in society as a whole. Thus the nature of the

46

status system in any formal organization is largely determined by the notions of class and caste governing the needs and desires of those whose behavior constitutes the formal organization. Hence, a comprehensive treatment of the subject would logically begin with the study of status in the general social system. Some of this background has been provided in the preceding chapter. The present inquiry is restricted to the relatively simple study of the general facts about status systems in formal organizations, and the functions that such systems serve in such organizations.

The analysis to be presented herein is based upon experience and observation of the kind commonly understood by those who have organizing and executive experience, but it does not purport to express a consensus of opinion. It sets forth that systems of status in formal organizations are necessary as a matter of need of individuals, and as imposed by the characteristics of cooperative systems, especially with respect to the techniques of communication essential to coordination. But it also appears that systems of status generate uncontrolled and even uncontrollable tendencies to rigidity, hypertrophy, and unbalance that often lead to destruction of organization.

The scheme of presentation is as follows: (I) The nature and technical apparatus of status systems; (II) the functions of status systems with respect to individuals; (III) the functions of status in cooperative systems; and (IV) the destructive tendencies of systems of status.

I. THE NATURE AND TECHNICAL APPARATUS OF SYSTEMS OF STATUS IN FORMAL ORGANIZATIONS

By "status" of an individual in an organization we mean in the present text that condition of the individual that is defined by a statement of his rights, privileges, immunities, duties, and obligations in the organization and, obversely, by a statement of the restrictions, limitations, and prohibitions governing his behavior, both determining the expectations of others in reference thereto. Status becomes systematic in an organization when appropriate recognition of assigned status becomes the duty and the practice of all participating and when the conditions of the status of all individuals are published by means of differentiating designations, titles, appellations, insignia, or overt patterns of behavior.

Two kinds of systems of status may be discriminated, both being simultaneously observed in nearly all organizations and being partly overlapping and interdependent. The first kind, which we shall call *functional* systems of status, is that in which status does not depend upon authority and jurisdiction but upon function. The ranks are vertically divided into lateral groups of different callings, trades, crafts, métiers, divisions of labor, specializations, and professions. One common characteristic of them all is that authority of command of one over another is lacking or is irrelevant at least to the functional status. But this does not mean that functional statuses are equally valued. On the contrary, the variation is wide, from the "low" of common, unskilled, and casual labor, intermittently attached to organizations, to the "high," *e.g.*, of the expert accountant, lawyer, architect, physician, and clergyman. Though lateral differentiation of status is not confined to formal organizations, it is a characteristic of such organizations generally and especially of the larger organizations conspicuous for their elaborate divisions of labor.

Functional status is a general attribute. For example, merely performing carpentering at a given place, which would determine specific status varying for each individual from time to time and from place to place, is not what we mean by functional status. The "carpenter" is presumed by all to have certain capacities regardless of who he is or what he is doing and conversely is presumed to have limitations, *e.g.*, he is not authorized to give medical advice. It is the presumption of capacities and limitations without necessary regard to the immediate concrete activities of the individual that is the essential feature of systematic status. The emphasis is upon the potentialities of behavior, not necessarily upon the immediately observable behavior.

In the second kind of status system, which we shall call the *scalar*, status is determined by (1) the relationship of superiority or subordination in a chain of command or formal authority and (2) by jurisdiction. In this kind of status system the primary relationships are customarily conceived as being along vertical lines, of above and below, of superior and subordinate. Status is distinguished by horizontal levels, and integration is by vertical groups, several such groups exemplifying a "pyramid of authority." It should be noted that status is a general attribute of an individual associated with the occupation of a usually rather narrowly restricted position. For example, a naval captain possesses certain prerogatives not enjoyed by those of inferior rank and is deemed qualified for positions for which those of inferior rank will not ordinarily be acceptable; but the position of command actually occupied at a given time will be confined to a particular ship or shore station or staff position, and the immediate authority and responsibility will be correspondingly restricted.

Although the status systems of general societies will not be treated in this paper, the close interrelation of general social status and status in organizations should be noted. Where in a general society a low status is assigned based, *e.g.*, on race, nationality, sex, age, education, ownership of property, or family, it is difficult in general to acquire high status in formal organizations in that society; and where there is high social status it tends to facilitate attainment of high organization status, though less so in democratic than in aristocratic societies. Conversely, those having low status in a formal organization are not likely to have high social status, though there are many exceptions; and those having high status, especially in important organizations, tend thereby to acquire higher general social status. The bearing of this is that if status systems are necessary in formal organizations, it is probable that they will extend into general social relationships, in greater or less degree, depending upon the society.[1]

Nearly all members of formal organizations may be observed to be much preoccupied with matters of status; and the leaders or managers of such organizations are almost constantly concerned with problems of status for reasons that will be treated in some detail later. But to fix more clearly what we mean by status, it seems desirable to present briefly here the organization apparatus by which status is established and maintained. This apparatus may be described as of the following categories: (1) ceremonies of induction and appointment; (2) insignia and other public indicia of status; (3) titles and appellations of office and calling; (4) emoluments and perquisites of position and office; (5) limitations and restrictions of calling and office.

1. The use of ceremonies of induction and appointment varies widely in different types of organizations. Ceremonial induction is common to all grades and ranks in military and religious organizations, is quite widely used in governmental and educational organizations, and is almost absent in business organizations (at least in the United States).

---

[1] During the last several generations when scalar organizations were developing rapidly in Germany, organization status was carried over widely into generalized status in German society, formally, *i.e.*, by title. See PARSONS, TALCOTT, "Democracy and Social Structure in Pre-Nazi Germany," *Journal of Legal and Political Sociology*, November, 1942.

2. Insignia and other indicia of status are nearly universal in military organization, especially in time of war, and in many religious organizations, especially as to the clergy. They are also used in many educational organizations on ceremonial occasions. They are little used in civil governmental organizations (except by the departments for police and fire protection) or in business organizations except for the wearing of union labor insignia in many trades and, in Europe, distinctive garb for those employed in some trades.

3. Titles and appellations of address are universal in formal organizations both for scalar and for functional status. In the case of functional status the title often begins as a mere designation of the function performed, as "clerk," "bookkeeper," "lineman," "typesetter," etc., and initially has no implication of systematic status; but very quickly, since classification by functions is attended by other distinguishing conditions such as differences in compensation, such titles become also the designations of status.

4. Emoluments, perquisites, and privileges are highly important evidences of status and are often highly valued. Care should be taken, however, to distinguish between the valuation of them as material rewards and as evidences and elements of status. They are almost universally employed in organizations of all kinds. In business and in some other organizations they are even more important than titles in fixing status. The use or nonuse of restricted quarters, automobiles, chauffeurs, private offices, private secretaries, and other perquisites in various combinations, time clocks, etc., provide a complex code that describes the system of status in effect, thoroughly understood by the initiated and fairly easily sensed by the outside observer.

5. Both higher and lower statuses are also established and published by restrictions and limitations of behavior that relate almost exclusively to maintenance and protection of status and the status system. For example, those of higher

status often cannot go to places where those of lower status are free to go, or do things that those of lower status may do, or say things or use language, etc. Though this is well understood, these limitations are not often made explicit and they are among the most subtle elements of status systems.

This, it is hoped, is sufficient to make clear the nature and in general the technical features of systems of status in scalar organizations so far as necessary for present purposes. If so, we may proceed to the main business of studying the functions and the consequences of such systems.

II. The Functions of Systems of Status with Respect to Individuals

Systems of status of different kinds and of various degrees of elaborateness and complexity are found in most if not all formal organizations. The establishing of a nucleus of such a system is one of the very first steps in creating an organization.[1] Are these facts merely reflections of habitual attitudes and needs transferred from general society and coming down from antiquity? The view to be developed here is that systems of status, though they may be affected in degrees and in details by habitual attitudes and needs projected from the customary beliefs of people, are fundamentally determined by the necessities associated with the needs and interests of individuals as biological and social units; and upon the requirements arising from the physical and social limitations inherent in systems of cooperation. In the

---

[1] In the case of corporations, corporation law provides at least often for both boards of directors and for two or more general officers. Bylaws almost always provide for additional general officers. In the case of individually owned businesses and partnerships the nucleus of the status system rests initially directly upon property ownership. Similarly with noncommercial organizations, the first steps in organizing are likely to be to create an initial governing board and a set of officers.

present section we shall deal with the relation of status systems to the needs of individuals.

It may be asserted first of all that systems of status arise from the differential needs, interests, and capacities of individuals. I shall discuss these in five topical divisions, as follows:

1. The differences in the *abilities* of individuals.

2. The differences in the *difficulties* of doing various kinds of work.

3. The differences in the *importance* of various kinds of work.

4. The desire for formal status as a social or organizational tool.

5. The need for protection of the integrity of the person.

1

Differences of ability with respect to any kind of effort in which there is social interest obviously lead to a recognition of difference of status of individuals in respect to that kind of effort. This does not necessarily imply superiority or inferiority in general, although, in fact, usually the lack of capacity of individuals for most kinds of effort or even for any valued effort whatsoever does inescapably establish for them a general position of at least technical or productive inferiority.

Differences of ability among individuals arise from a variety of conditions. The most obvious and possibly the most important are physiological or anatomical conditions, either inherent in the constitution of the individual from birth or imposed later by accident or disease. Cases of extreme physical or mental incapacity or even partial incapacity require no comment.[1] There are also some very im-

---

[1] The importance of such limitations in a population is commonly disregarded. Among adults probably not less than 1 in 20, or 5 per cent, is to be so classified.

portant differences such as lethargic constitution, slowness of reactions, and lack of curiosity as contrasted with vigor, alertness, quickness of reaction, natural accuracy of physical coordination, and active curiosity. The latter characteristics or their lack when manifested in early years are especially important as affecting the capacity to receive instruction and other social conditioning and to acquire experience. Differences that are small or deemed unimportant in early years thus may cumulate to be substantial at maturity or at the end of the most active learning period.

Other differences of capacity so obviously depend upon education and specialized training that little need be said on this subject. Broadly considered, it includes the social conditioning attendant upon living in a social milieu. Differences in education come from differences in ability to receive instruction and from differences in interest; hence, from differences in willingness to accept the discipline and sacrifices involved; from differences in economic and social resources; and from differences in the educational resources available.

Finally, differences of individual ability arise from differences of experience. Physical, social, and intellectual skills develop through practice. There appears to be a considerable degree of chance in the distribution of opportunities for experience. There is also wide variation in the disposition to adhere to a long course of experience, to "stick to one job." Again, there is considerable variation in the capacity to learn from experience, *i.e.*, in the faculty of self-education.

Such differences among individuals as are here outlined do not prove the necessity of formal systems of status; nor that, if they imply such formal systems in some respects, they involve a formal qualification or disqualification in all respects. They do suggest that the first base upon which status systems rest is the undeniable differences, whatever their origins, between the physical, mental, and social capacities and interests of individuals. It will be recognized that these are fundamental conditions of immediate practical and inescapable significance, *e.g.*, to the teacher, the military officer, or the employer.

2

Differences in the capacities of individuals undoubtedly lead to differences of informal status quite aside from the requirements of formal organizations. For example, some groups tend to form on the basis of educational level, or physical strength, or endurance, etc. But the important significance of differences of ability stems from differences in the nature of various kinds of activities. Many kinds of work, unskilled labor, for example, usually require only sound health and normal physiological abilities. Other work, say that of a laboratory chemist, may require unusual delicacy of physiological reaction in the use of laboratory equipment, long arduous technical education, powers of imagination, thorough experience, and a willingness to work persistently without supervision or instruction. The work requires an exceptional combination of powers, some of which may need to be developed to an exceptional degree. Recognition of the status of being exceptional is forced upon such a man by his own experience. He is made aware of it by the difficulty of finding those competent to carry on his work or to assist him. He is also elevated to exceptional status by those who wish his work to be done and who find that there are few competent to do it. Those whose interests are narrowly concentrated in one field for this reason often regard exceptional ability in that field as indicating not only special but general superiority. The banker finding few who can function effectively in his field, whatever their condition of education and experience, may be led to believe that those who can do so are of status generally superior to all others. A broader view, of course, recognizes that great superiority in one field does not imply general superiority.

Thus the second base for status is, as contrasted with personal ability, the relative difficulty of things to be done. The difficulties will usually be appraised on judgment based on general experience and observation; or, more objectively, on the basis of the numbers or proportions of individuals who can or cannot do well the various tasks.

3

The exceptional ability to do things that are exceptionally difficult, while it is a sufficient basis for establishing differences of status in the general estimation, is not sufficient to establish a *system* of status involving authority or responsibility. Superiority in formal organizations depends upon exceptional ability for exceptionally difficult work of exceptional *importance*. "Importance" in this context includes more than economic importance. High status is not accorded to superior ability to do unusually difficult things of trivial character, except perhaps in very restricted circles. On the contrary, if an activity is regarded as exceptionally important, even though not very difficult, superior status is nevertheless likely to be accorded to superior ability with respect to it. This is probably most evident in the economic world, but it is readily seen in other spheres, *e.g.*, in military organization.

The importance of the work, then, establishes the importance of the position that "seeks" those of exceptional ability. Relative difficulty is a factor but is usually of minor importance except when importance is approximately equal. Status becomes systematic because activities regarded as important are systematized and organized.

4

The next basis for status is pragmatic. Insignia and titles of status have the effect of credentials. They create a presumption with respect to the character, ability, and specific skills or functions of individuals. They are not conclusive, of course, but as preliminaries, as introductions, they save time and prevent awkwardness and embarrassment. The general's stars indicate at a glance the nature of his responsibilities and the probable relative reliability of his utterances in certain fields. The title "M.D." creates a presumption that the holder of that degree may usefully be approached without reticence about bodily ills. The degree of "Ph.D." may be granted to a fool, but very generally it is a sign of the possession of a considerable intellectual experience, scholarly or scientific skill, and mental discipline. "Vice-president" of a corporation indicates one who probably understands business language and organization. "Foreman" indicates the man through whom the most effective approach may probably be had respecting the group under him and the work they are doing. "Bishop" is the title of one whom the communicant may accept as having certain ecclesiastical responsibilities and authority and as being able to perform certain spiritual functions, though the communicant may never before have seen him or been told about him.

Generally, the possession of title and of other indicia of rank certifies that those in the best position to have responsible judgment acknowledge and publish the status indicated, which all whom it may concern may accept at least tentatively. The convenience and efficiency of the status system is such that men seek status as a necessary tool in their work; and for the same reasons it is imposed upon them by those responsible for their work. It is to be noted that this applies as much to functional status as it does to scalar status.

5

Insofar as systems of status are imposed "from the top" they are expressions of the requirements of coordination rather than of the ambitions of the most able and powerful acting on the basis of personal motives. The personal motivation of most profound effect, applying equally to those of superior and to those of inferior status, is the need for protecting the integrity of the person in a social environment. This leads some to seek superior formal status, but it also leads others to refuse superior status and even to seek inferior status, depending upon the individual and the circumstances. This may be demonstrated sufficiently by presenting four modes in which the need for status is expressed: (*a*) The need of integrating personal history by the conferring of status; (*b*) the need of imputing superior status to those from whom commands are to be received; (*c*) the need of imputing superior status as a means of symbolizing possession of personal value in participating in an organization; and (*d*) the need of status as a protection against excessive claims against the individual.

a. The need of integrating one's personal history into one's personality by the attainment of improved status and by the conferring of status publicly is exceptionally important to those who by deliberate effort or sacrifice condition themselves to the possession of superior knowledge, skill, or experience. The need is for an endorsement of the individual's past history as a creditable element in his existing personality. The granting and attainment of improved or different status here is not reward but anointment. It serves a ceremonial function of announcement, of proclamation, that an approved course has been followed by this person. Without such endorsement the effort often appears to the individual to have been in vain. A sense of frustration, sometimes devastating, may follow. Even when the individual is one of extraordinary self-sufficiency, the attainment of recognized distinction of status may be desired to maintain standing with relatives and supporting and cooperating friends. No one who watches the contemporary parade of diplomas, degrees, public honors, and the award of innumerable insignia of achievement and distinction, and who observes the reaction of individuals, of families, of organizations, and of the public to them can doubt the importance of these recognitions in nearly every field of individual and social activity. If such distinctions, often of ephemeral value, are an important element in individual behavior, it is evident that permanent position of status is even more so. It may be thought that the need of status here discussed is merely a reflection of the effect of attitudes, inculcated by mores and institutions that no doubt do reinforce the need; but the response of small children to status and the use made of status in instruction and discipline of the very young suggest that the need is more primitive and is individual.

b. The need of imputing higher status to those from whom commands come is rather certain though it is not often obvious. It is apparent to nearly everyone on the basis of even simple and limited experience that the coordination of effort necessary for effective cooperation can be practically secured only by specializing the function of command. It is obvious that everybody cannot give orders to everybody else at the same time and for the same activity. But except at times of great danger, to receive orders from a nondescript "some-other" is felt to be an injury to the self-respect, to the integrity, of the person. This can be avoided or alleviated only if it is felt that command is exercised by "right" either conferred by supernatural authority; or, more generally in our present society, conferred by superior ability; or by the burden of superior responsibility. Men are eager to be "bossed" by superior ability, but they resent being bossed by men of no greater ability than they themselves have. So strong is this need of assigning superior status to those in positions of command that, unless the obvious facts preclude it, men will impute abilities they cannot recognize or judge. They want to believe that those of higher au-

thority "know what they are doing" when they appoint someone over them. Since men in the ranks are not capable of
judging or are not in a position in advance to judge the competence of men in posts of command remote from them by
two or more grades or even of those in immediate command
if special technical abilities are required (*e.g.*, the surgeon
in the operating room or the navigator of a ship), this desire
for the justification of subordination leads often to profuse
rationalization about status and even to mythological and
mystical explanations of it; but the ways in which a need is
manifested ought not to be permitted to obscure its nature
or the function of the means that satisfy it.

What has just been said as respects the need of imputing
higher scalar status to those from whom commands are received applies somewhat less definitely and more subtly to
differences in functional status where authoritative advice
rather than formal authority is involved. Thus the advice
or even the directions of one having the status of an expert
in a particular field will be accepted against that of someone
recognized as being equally expert but not having status.
The subjective factor involved may be that of a diffuse feeling of public authorization to transfer responsibility to one
having functional status. Though there is wide variation in
the competence of those having the same status and reliance
upon mere formal status is subject to much error and abuse,
nevertheless there can be little doubt that the system of functional status affords great relief to nearly everybody in practical everyday social behavior.

c. The need felt by those of subordinate rank for imputing personal superiority to those in command, *i.e.*, the
need of protecting the integrity of the person, is also expressed in sentiments of valuation of an organization as a
whole. To be a member of a good organization is a personal
asset. It is among the claims to distinction of most men. To
be ejected from an organization is a serious, sometimes a

catastrophic, injury to the integrity of the person. "Patriotism," "sense of communion," "loyalty," *"esprit de corps"* are common expressions of this attitude. Few, if any, with experience of command will doubt this, and those who observe behavior of men in military organizations in war know how powerful and indispensable this sentiment is, though perhaps not many would express the facts in terms of personal integrity.

One of the effects of this need is to sustain the system of status. For if it is not practicable for all to command, and command, *i.e.*, coordination, is essential to organization, then a system of status is indispensable. Office becomes symbolic of the organization. The commander in chief not only occupies the supreme position of command, but he speaks for the army and in his person symbolizes it.

d. Individuals of superior ability and those of inferior ability can comfortably work together only on a basis of physical or social segregation. If no formal segregation is established, either friction and noncooperation occur or there is spontaneous informal segregation, "natural" leaders leading "natural" groups, without being adequately integrated into the system of formal command. The necessity for differentiation from the standpoint of those of inferior ability is that without it they are constantly in a position of disadvantage, under pressure to exceed their capacities, perpetually losing in a race in which no handicaps are recognized, never able to attain expected goals so long as they are treated as the equals of those who are in fact superior; therefore they are always in a position of never securing respect for what they do contribute, of always incurring disrespect for what they cannot do. Men cannot stand this kind of inferiority and its frustrations. The inferiors will group themselves and command respect by various means if they are not protected by being assigned a formal status, which, though inferior, recognizes their position as being more or less indispensable and participating even though individually less important. The practice of labor unions of restraining the production of the more able workers of an undifferentiated craft to a level approximating that of the poorer workers, though in practice doubtless of complex motivation, seems clearly in accordance with the human needs of the situation.

Concordantly, the abler individuals press for segregation corresponding to the observed differences in abilities and in contributions. To be lumped in with inferiors in ability seems an unjust withholding of recognition, an injury to the integrity of the person. Their escape from this position will probably be more individualistic than that of those of inferior abilities who must more often resort to group solidarity. One escape or attempt to escape for the superior individual is to try to organize the group, to adopt a function of leadership, or to dominate without authority. Another is to leave the group for various alternative activities—found a new sect, start a new business, establish a party, and so on.

Much experience demonstrates that those who are unequal cannot work well for long as equals. But experience also demonstrates that where differences of status are recognized formally, men of very unequal abilities and importance can and do work together well for long periods.

This discussion of the relationship of integrity of the person to systems of status is not exhaustive or comprehensive, but it is enough to suggest that personal need of status system is one of their foundations.

III. The Functions of Status in Cooperative Systems

Up to this point the approach to systems of status has been in terms of the characteristics of human beings and their bearing on behavior and fundamental relationships in formal systems of cooperation. The differences in abilities arising from biological characteristics and from social conditioning and experience; the variation in the difficulties of work; the variations in importance of work; the systematic character of cooperation arising from valuation of effort; the common sense of the necessity of centralizing and specializing the function of command; the need of formalizing differences of status to protect the integrity of the socialized individual; and the symbolic functions of systems of status—all of this may be taken as the basis of the evolution of systems of status. The patterns may be as unplanned or undevised, as "spontaneous" or "instinctive" as languages. But having been evolved, they have been subjected to observation and analysis and deliberate modification, development, and design in much the same way that old languages are to some degree modified by intention and new languages have been constructed. Executives have to have a practical understanding of systems of status and are persistently occupied with concrete operations of selection, appointment, changes of status, modification of hierarchical relationships, inculcation of doctrines of command or management, and ceremonial activities, all directed to maintaining and improving the system of status and assuring that it performs its function in coordinating behavior. Much of the theory stated above appears to be sensed by executives, though not necessarily comprehended intellectually and not made explicit. The observations of practical executives would not be in terms of social psychology but in the technical terms of specific organization practice and forces.

Proceeding, then, on this level of discourse it appears necessary to the executive to recognize by some formal means differences in the ability of individuals and differences in the importance of their work or of their contribution to cooperative effort. However, executives are probably much more conscious of the necessity of systems of status as (1) a function of the system of organization communication, the fundamental process in cooperation; (2) as an important part of the system of incentives; and (3) as an essential means of inculcating and developing a sense of responsibility and of imposing and fixing responsibility.

1

A system of organization communication, in order that it may operate with sufficient accuracy and rapidity, has to be so designed that it may easily and quickly be assured that particular communications are (*a*) authentic, (*b*) authoritative, and (*c*) intelligible.

a. Under ordinary circumstances, and especially with respect to routine matters, explicit authentication of communications is not required. Personal acquaintance with or knowledge of the communicator together with the relevance of the communication to the general context and to previous communications are sufficient. The status system is not of great importance in this connection. But in times of emergency and great danger or in respect to important matters, explicit authentication of communications often becomes necessary. Witnessed written communications or letterheads indicating the name, position, and title of the communicator and personal introductions by mutually known third parties are among the means used. There is no doubt that here the status system greatly facilitates authentication—it is one of the practical uses of insignia of office.

b. It is in respect to the authoritativeness of a communication, however, that we find the basic need for systems of status. The primary question of the recipient of a communication, assuming that it is authentic, *i.e.*, comes from whom it purports to come, is whether the contents of the communication may be relied upon as a basis for action. This is what we mean by authoritativeness. Authoritativeness in this context is of two kinds: functional authoritativeness; and scalar or command authoritativeness.

Whether a communication reflects the facts and needs of the situation depends upon whether the individual (or body) that emits it has the general qualifications for understanding what he (or it) communicates about and whether he is *in a position* to have the essential concrete knowledge.

A report from a carpenter about the condition of a generator in a power house is initially not credible; that of the electrician in charge is credible, though not conclusive; that of an electric power engineer is more credible and *may* be accepted as final. The authoritativeness of the report depends in part upon the qualifications of those reporting, and these are presumptively established by formal status. But a report by an electrician in Des Moines about a generator in New York is not credible. He has the qualifications in general, but he is not in a position to apply them to the situation in New York.

The purpose of the report may be to secure help in the correction of some fault. The help needed may be in the form of superior technical instruction; it may be in the form of the application of some maintenance skill or of a replacement part. The electrician is not in a position to know the status of those whose services are needed. His superior does —he knows less of the concrete situation, but he has more technical knowledge or more knowledge of the relevant status system.

The functional status system is so extraordinarily convenient in providing prima-facie evidence of the authoritativeness of communications that we depend upon it almost exclusively in the conduct of daily affairs generally as well as in all organizations. It does not imply any generalized superiority or inferiority of status in this aspect. It does not exclude discrimination as between individuals having the same status, nor does it assume errors may not occur in relying upon the prima-facie evidence granted by status. The plumber, or electrician, or lawyer, or doctor may be immature or poor or even bad, as determined by experience or surmised from observation; but even so may often be presumed to be superior to those of other statuses. A poor doctor, even though inadequate, will generally be a better advisor on medical matters than an expert plumber. Systematized functional status would seem to be absolutely indispensable for the effective operation of complex divisions of labor, and it may also be indispensable even for relatively simple divisions of labor, although in the latter condition there may be some acceptable "jacks of all trade."

c. The special system of status associated with chains of command or hierarchy of authority depends upon each position being a "communication center," the inferior command being associated with restricted areas or fields, the higher command being more comprehensive. Outside the technical competence special to each field of organization, the general functions common to all hierarchies of command are: to evaluate the meaning of communications received in the form of advices and reports, largely affected by the status of the transmitter; to know to whom communications should be relayed (*i.e.*, to know the relevant status system or "the organization"); to select that which needs to be relayed; and to translate communications, before relaying, into language appropriate to the receiver.

The system of command communication cannot effectively work except on the basis of a status system. For very small organizations communication may effectively be addressed to persons, but for larger systems status becomes primary. Contrast saying to the new office boy, "Take this order to Bill Jones in building K" (in which there are two Bill Joneses) and "Take this order to the foreman of section 12 in the Y Department in building K." Contrast the following orders: "Capt. Jones of Station Y and Capt. Smith of

Station X will advise each other by telephone each morning as to their respective situations and will advise Major Allen of any unusual circumstances." "The Commandants of Station X and Y will advise each other and this office each morning of their respective situations and of any unusual circumstances." In the first case any change of personalities calls for a new order—otherwise the desired collaboration will fail.

Although both functional and scalar systems of status are essential to establishing in a practicable degree the authoritativeness of communications, authoritativeness is not sufficient. Unless communications are intelligible they cannot be acted upon correctly or effectively. Now, it is apparent that the intelligibility of a communication depends not merely upon the capacity of the communicator but also upon that of the receiver. Thus communications of the same content will differ very greatly, depending upon the status of those to whom they are addressed. Whether a communication is intelligible depends upon the use of language having the same meaning to the originator and to the receiver of the communication. This requires a selection of language, depending upon from whom and to whom the communication is made. Systems of status are an indispensable guide to the selection of appropriate language.

Thus in the power-house illustration above, if the electrician makes his report to the engineer it will be phrased differently than if made to some different official or to an outside layman. But the electrician is presumably not adept at translation to meet a wide variety of communication needs. His superior is presumably more adept.

When communications are sent from a subordinate to his superior it is called a report. When it is sent from the superior to the subordinate and is in peremptory terms it is a command or order. The difference is superficial. The command implies the following report: "From my superior position I report that the situation calls for the following action on your part." Very often in fact it is in the form: The situation as known to us here is so and so; it permits you to use your own judgment, based on the local situation, *i.e.*, issue the orders to yourself.

The executive, then, is much preoccupied with systems of status because they are important in the authentication of communications, indispensable in establishing a working presumption of the authoritativeness of their content, and essential to their intelligibility.

2

Systems of status are also important because maintenance of status and improvement of status are among the essential incentives to cooperation. The scarcity of effective incentives calls for use of many kinds of incentives; and their wise use requires, especially in larger organizations, their systematic use.

Status as an incentive has two aspects suggested earlier. The first is that of prestige for its own sake, as a reinforcement of the ego, as security for the integrity of the person. This is an important need of many individuals. They will work hard to satisfy it and forego much to attain it. The second aspect is that of prestige as a valuable or indispensable means to other ends. Thus some men endure publicity or accept conspicuous positions of onerous character as a means of supporting organizations or of eliciting the support of others because they like philanthropic, or scientific, or cultural work, which is their fundamental incentive.

The importance of status as an incentive is shown by the immense amount of work and sacrifice made by innumerable volunteer heads of social, philanthropic, religious, political, and scientific organizations. For some the motive is directly personal. For others it is the "good of the cause" and the

personal incentive is satisfaction in the promotion of that
cause.

These are perhaps the most obvious instances of the importance of status as incentive. The executive is frequently
concerned with the instances where material rewards are by
themselves ineffective and status proves to be the controlling
or a necessary supplementary incentive. He is also concerned with the still less conspicuous cases where prestige
is a negative incentive, where preferred status is regarded as
too burdensome, and where it is believed to be a limitation on
personal liberties.

3

The system of status is a strong and probably an indispensable developer of the sense of responsibility and therefore of stability and reliability. Loss of status is more than
loss of its emoluments; it is more than loss of prestige. It is
a serious injury to the personality. Thus while improvement of status is important, especially to the more able, and
desirable to many, loss of status is much more generally re-
sisted. It is difficult to accept, or to be accepted in, a reduced status. Indeed, the fear of losing status is what leads
some to refuse advancement of status. The desire for improvement of status and especially the desire to protect
status appears to be the basis of the sense of general responsibility. Responsibility is established and enforced by
specific penalties for specific failures and by limitation of
status or by loss of a particular status for failure in general.
Although both methods in conjunction are most effective, of
the two it would appear that the second is much more effective than the first, especially as to those above low levels of
status. In view of the extreme importance of dependable
behavior, the function of status in creating and maintaining dependable behavior is probably indispensable. The
extent of criminal behavior suggests that specific sanctions

are not sufficient in general to establish adequate responsibility.

We have now completed an abbreviated presentation of rationale of status systems universally found in scalar organizations. What has been set forth may well be summarized before we proceed to consider the disruptive tendencies inherent in them.

Status systems have their origins in differences in the biological and socially acquired characteristics of individuals, in differences in the difficulties of the various kinds of activities, and in differences in the valuation of these activities. Systems of status are a means of protecting the integrity of the person, especially of those of inferior ability. Superior status is often necessary to the effectiveness of the work of those of superior ability. All this is on the level of biology and social psychology. Additional observations on the level of sociology and the technique of organization show that systems of status are necessary to specialization of function; that they are essential to the system of organization communications for purposes of coordination; that they are important and sometimes indispensable as affording incentives; and that they are important in promoting the sense of responsibility and, therefore, the dependability and stability essential to cooperation. These inductions from experience and observation and from history are not scientific proof of the theory outlined; but they are believed to present a fair basis, of considerable probability of correctness, for the assertion that systems of status are not the product of irrational mores, mythologies, and rationalizations, but are specific modes of adaptation of behavior to fundamental characteristics of individuals and to the fundamental physical, biological, and social properties of systems of scalar organization.

IV. Disruptive Tendencies Inherent in Status Systems

The concern of executives is not only with the organizing functions of systems of status, but with their disruptive tendencies; for, paradoxically, such systems operate like principles of growth, necessary to attain maturity, but without a self-regulative control that prevents disproportionate development of parts, unbalance, and maladaptation to the environment. Thus, the executive who promotes by positive means an improved system of status, however essential to immediate purposes, thereby generates disorganizing forces, the neutralizing of which is the more difficult in that the executive himself is a central part of the system of status. Thus the effort to detect and correct hypertrophy and abuse of the status system is somewhat akin to correcting psychopathic difficulties by introspection. Nevertheless, some executives, being individuals as well as officials, are undoubtedly able to project themselves mentally to a position outside their organizations and to view it with detachment. They then can recognize that a system of status presents a persistent dilemma.

The pathological aspects of systems of status to which these remarks refer have not been adequately investigated. We shall focus our consideration of the subject on the following topics:

1. The status system tends in time to distorted evaluation of individuals.

2. It restricts unduly the "circulation of the elite."

3. It distorts the system of distributive justice.

4. It exaggerates administration to the detriment of leadership and morale.

5. It exalts the symbolic function beyond the level of sustainment.

6. It limits the adaptability of an organization.

1

As set forth hereinbefore, the system of status is founded on and made necessary by the following four factors, in addition to others, relevant to the present topic: (*a*) differences in the abilities of individuals, (*b*) differences in the difficulties of various kinds of work, (*c*) differences in the importance of various kinds of work, and (*d*) the needs of the system of communication.

The first of these factors is strictly personal and individual. This does not mean, of course, that the capacities of the individual may not have been largely determined socially, but that at any given time they are the personal possession of the individual and that the application or non-application of these capacities at any given time or period is taken to be a matter of personal choice or will. To the extent that status depends upon individual ability and willingness to employ it, it may be said to be individual and not social. Personal status may to this extent be said to be correlative with personal merit. Undoubtedly, evaluation from this point of view is widely conceived as just. If this were the only basis of status, it seems probable that differences of status would be accepted as proper and necessary even where material distribution could be conceived as properly made on the basis of "to each according to need."

As we ascend to the other bases of status, more and more qualification of the conception of individual merit is required. Thus the differences in the difficulties of tasks are in some degree merely matters of the nature of the physical world and of the capacities of individuals; but where acquired skills and technologies are involved, being almost entirely of social origin, relative difficulties indirectly are socially determined. Further, almost every task in a formal society involves adaptation of behavior to and utilization of the social system itself. What is rated as easy or difficult

72

behavior is socially evaluated. Hence, individual merit in performing the difficult often lies in capacity and willingness to resign personal preferences. The qualification on account of the social element in "difficult" is not important. "Difficult" reflects a social standard of measurement of abilities; the standard and the abilities together are a basis for status.

Variations in the *importance* of work as a basis for status are quite another matter. "Importance" is almost entirely determined socially in the same sense, though not necessarily in the same way, that economic value is determined by demand and supply as socially expressed, *i.e.*, in exchange. To the extent that the individual accepts the social valuation and does that which is regarded as important, there is personal merit. Whether the status accorded is inferior or superior, however, will depend upon whether those able and willing are relatively numerous or not. Thus, low status frequently acompanies work of primary importance in the aggregate, *e.g.*, wheat growing, in which numerous individuals are employed; high status often accompanies work which *in the aggregate* is relatively unimportant, but scarce, hence valuable, *e.g.*, silversmithing.

The rating of the individual by the importance of his work, a social evaluation, may be necessary to effective and efficient allocation of ability in the social system, and it may therefore be essential to the adaptation of the society as a whole to its environment. However, status so determined tends, as experience shows, to be imputed to the individual *as such* rather than to a particular socially valued *role* of the individual. When inferior status is assigned on this basis, it is transferred to the individual generally, and similarly when superior status is assigned. Thus exaggeration of personal inferiority and superiority results. The effect upon the characteristics of the individual contributors to an organization is deleterious—depressing and limiting those of inferior status, stimulating and sometimes intoxicating those of superior status. Restoring or creating morale in the one, restraining the other, then becomes a major problem of organization.

The system of communication by means of which coordination is secured in cooperation is a strictly social phenomenon. Being indispensable to purposeful cooperation, the necessities of the system of communication become prime, being secondary only to the prior existence of an organization whose members are willing to cooperate. Now, undoubtedly the capacity of individuals to function in a system of communications depends upon natural abilities, general knowledge and experience, facility in general and special languages, technical and other special abilities; but though often indispensable, such general capacities and potentialities are secondary to the abilities directly associated with a particular communication position and with immediate concrete knowledge. One cannot function as or in a communication center if one is not at that center; nor, if at that center, without knowledge of the immediately available means of communication and of the immediately precedent communication materials, *i.e.*, what has just transpired, what further communication is called for, to whom and where further communication should be made, from whom and where communication should be elicited. Neither general nor special abilities suffice to meet the requirements if this local and concrete knowledge is not available.

Thus the primary specific abilities required in communication are those of *position*—of being at the place where communication may effectively be had and where immediate concrete knowledge may be obtained. The manning of posts of communication by those possessing the requisite abilities of position is so indispensable to cooperation that a system assuring such manning and hence of the acquirement of such abilities has precedence over all other considerations in an organization, for the breakdown of communication means immediate failure of coordination and disintegration of organization. It should not be understood from this that the general capacities and abilities of individuals are not important. If positions of communication are not manned by those of requisite general and special abilities, other than ability of position, disintegration of organization occurs slowly through failure to accomplish the aims of cooperation in ways that permit the satisfaction of the motives of the contributing individuals of an organization. The analogy is that of starvation by malnutrition as against death by trauma, such as the severing of an essential nerve. The logical as well as the instinctively acceptable choice is to avoid fatal accident even at the expense of serious and dangerous limitations; for fatal injury admits of no recovery, whereas the tendency toward dissolution even when regarded as probably certain, admits of the possibility of reversal.

It may be seen from the foregoing that schemes ensuring continuity of ordered communication are of primary importance in the adaptation of a society to its environment as well as to the attainment of ends transcending mere biological adaptation. In the past, schemes for the manning of communication posts of society have been based upon heredity (feudal systems), heredity and marriage (kinship systems), systems of property rights, systems of commission and appointment, and systems of election. All of them create differential status essential to ordered communication. The failure of any of them prior to the acceptance of a substitute system disrupts communication, and hence leads to prompt disorganization.

The indispensability of systematic communication in organization thus leads to imputing a value to the individual that relates to the role he plays and to the exaggeration of the importance of immediate local ability in communication as against more general and more personal ability.

The dilemma involved may be brought out in terms of a practical organization problem. It will ordinarily be the experience of the general executive that there are able men available for appointment to positions occupied by men recognized to be of inferior ability, but who are immediately superior with respect to local knowledge and experience in their posts, and also superior in the sense that they are accepted in their posts by others. It may be clear that in the long run, provided immediate breakdown is not involved, it would be better to replace the inferior with the superior man. Nevertheless, to do so may involve costs in terms of immediate organizational disadvantages so substantial that the net effect even for the long run might be adverse. These disadvantages are: (*a*) If replacement is made, there will be ineptitude of functioning for a longer or shorter period. Insofar as this occurs because of lack of local knowledge, it will correct itself in time, which in general will be shorter the greater the general ability of the replacing individual. The less difference there is in ability, the more doubtful is the utility of change. (*b*) Communication involves mutual relationships and habitual responsive reactions. A new man entirely aside from his intrinsic abilities in the position, is new to others in the immediate communication network. *Their* capacity to function is disturbed by change. (*c*) The operation of the system depends in considerable degree upon mutual confidence of the communicators. Change decreases this confidence. This is ordinarily not important as related to single changes not frequently occurring. Its importance increases at an accelerating pace as either the number or the frequency of replacements increases.

2

Thus, although systems of status are based upon individual abilities and propensities as related to tasks socially evaluated and upon the requirements of the system of communication in organizations, we find that the rating of the individual by the role he occupies and emphasis upon the importance to the organization of immediate local abilities of position leads to under- and overvaluation of individuals artificially, *i.e.*, in terms of status as an end instead of as an intermediate means.

Whatever the system or principle by which posts of communication are filled, in general, errors occur, with the result that some men of inferior abilities are placed in relatively superior positions. Moreover, even if men at a given time were all placed with ideal correctness, they change so that some become inferior to their positions, and others become more than adequate for them. Further, changes in the conditions or the purposes of cooperation may make obsolete the capacities of individuals in particular positions for which they were initially well adapted. Finally, individuals will develop or mature whose abilities are superior to those of persons who have preferred status, even though the latter have not changed and at the time of selection were the best available. The effects of aging, of physical, moral, and intellectual deterioration, of changing conditions and purposes, all call for continual readjustment and replacement in the status system. The process of readjustment and replacement is well known as the "circulation of the elite." Ideally the circulation of the elite should be so free that the status of all should at any given time be in accordance with their relative capacities and the importance of their functions. It is rather obvious that failure of this circulation to the extent that generally those of inferior capacity occupy positions of superior status will so reduce the efficiency of cooperation that survival of organization is doubtful, and that the dangers of rebellion and revolution will be so great that even for the short run such a stoppage of circulation may be fatal.

Nevertheless, even a rough approach to the ideal condition

of free circulation is not possible. This is due to three essential factors: (*a*) A considerable degree of stability of status is necessary if improvement of status is to serve as an incentive. The more uncertain the retention of achieved status is, the fewer to whom the achievement of status will appeal. (*b*) The resistance to loss of status is in general stronger than desire to achieve higher status, so that it is often probable that the disruptive effects of demotion made to attain a more perfect assignment of capacities more than offset the advantages. (*c*) Good communication depends to a great extent upon accuracy of interpretation largely associated with habitual personal relationships. These are broken down if changes are frequent.

3

Without a system of status, as has already been stated, injustice results to those who are the less capable, by failure to protect them against overburden. If an adequate system of status is employed, it may involve injustice when the higher emoluments of higher status are greater than warranted in the sense that they are greater than necessary. It is not intended to discuss here the problem of distributive justice generally involved in differential emoluments. We shall assume that a differential system is necessary and just. What concerns us now is the distortions of justice arising from the retrictions upon freedom of promotion and demotion. The injustices arising are of two sorts: (*a*) The aggregate of emoluments of higher status are excessive in the sense that they do not secure the degree of service that the capacities ideally available make possible. The "social dividend" in the broadest sense is less than it should be, and the failure is a loss to those of inferior status generally. (*b*) Individuals capable of filling positions of higher status better than those occupying such positions are unjustly deprived of the emoluments that they are often encouraged to seek. I am using emoluments in a most general sense, including not only remuneration, but also recognition, prestige, the satisfaction of exercising one's abilities, and, for those of philanthropic motivation, the satisfactions of the largest service of which they are capable.

These injustices inherent in the practical operations of systems of status are not hidden. Men are aware of them in general and sometimes exaggerate them; and they are also aware of them specifically as affecting them individually in many circumstances. The effect of the sense of injustice involved depends partly upon the degree to which the status system is sluggish or congealed. When status is fixed by birth or limited by race or religion the extreme of disorganization may follow. When the status of individuals corresponds well with their abilities some loss of *esprit de corps* and of cooperative efficiency only may be involved.

Nevertheless, the effects of the injustices inherent in status systems are sufficiently great to require positive balancing considerations and sentiments. The consideration of most importance is that, except as to those of the lowest status (and at least in some conditions probably also to them)', conservatism is protective of individuals. Even though the retention of someone in a position of higher status may be felt to be specifically unjust to one of lower status, the situation may be duplicated with respect to the latter and someone of still lower status. In some degree recognition of a right to retain status is therefore felt to be generally just even though in particular cases the effect may be thought not so.

The sentiments supporting conservatism with respect to status are developed and maintained by rationalizations, ceremonies, and symbolism. They have for their broad purpose the inculcation of the doctrine that the primary interest of the individual is dependent upon the maintenance of the whole organization and its effective operation as a whole, and that whatever is necessary to this end, even though it adversely affects the individual, is offset even to him by the larger advantage accruing from it.

4

An effective system of communications requires not only the stable filling of specific positions of different status, but also habitual practices and technical procedures. Failure to follow these procedures with routine persistence in general leads to confusion, lack of coordination, and inefficiency or breakdown of the system. The lines of communication, the system of status, and the associated procedures, though by no means constituting "administration," are essential tools of administration and are the most "visible" general parts of it. Being the tangible machinery of administration and indispensable to it, the protection both of status and of procedure come to be viewed quite sincerely as the *sine qua non* of the organization.

The overvaluation of the apparatus of communication and administration is opposed to leadership and the development of leaders. It opposes leadership whose function is to promote appropriate adjustment of ends and means to new environmental conditions, because it opposes change either of status in general or of established procedures and habitual routine. This overvaluation also discourages the development of leaders by retarding the progress of the abler men and by putting an excessive premium on routine qualities.

5

Among the phenomena connected with the status system are symbols of office or of class or trade. In many cases these are not conspicuous, and may be only evident in matters of behavior, such as deference; in others, *e.g.*, military organizations, they are conspicuous. The investment of office with symbols is, moreover, often preceded by ceremonies of graduation, promotion, consecration, induction, installation, and inauguration, in which the organization and its purpose are dramatized and glorified by symbolic means. Much of this symbolic practice related to office in the abstract is transferred to the person of the individual filling the office, and in this way the individual himself by reason of his status becomes a symbol of the organization and of its purposes. This is so true that although it is usually not difficult to distinguish between personal and official acts *per se*, it is not acceptable in general to distinguish personal and official behavior of officials or for them to tolerate contumelious behavior of others toward them when wearing insignia of office or otherwise publicly known to hold office. Thus the rule is general that the private conduct of officials at least in public must not be "unbecoming a gentleman," though the rule is expressed in different manners and enforced in different degrees and in different ways. Conversely, an insult to an officer or person of other status publicly known as an officer or member of an organization is regarded as an injury to the organization itself, and especially so when committed by a member of the same organization.

This is rather evident and commonplace as respects clergymen, military personnel (in uniform), officers of the law, and judges when in courts. It is less obvious but nonetheless real in business, academic, and many other organizations where the symbols of office and status are primarily utilitarian, such as large office quarters, automobiles, guarded privacy, and special privileges.

One effect of the symbolic function of office and its associated status is to retard the circulation of the elite. The removal of an official to whom symbolic attributes have become attached, whether for incompetence or for other more reprehensible causes, unless they are very grave and publicly known, is widely felt to be derogatory to the office and to be an injury to the organization both internally and often externally as respects its prestige. Thus in one city some years ago it was said that it was practically impossible to discharge the presidents of banks except for flagrant, publicly known derelictions. Also it is often, not without ground, suspected that men are "kicked upstairs" to avoid the effects of crass degradation; and usually care and decorum is used. These considerations also in some cases explain and justify the provisions of pensions for officers under compulsory retirement rules.

Thus it comes about that the symbolism involved in office and status in the aggregate outruns the capacities of the men who have become symbols of organization.

6

From what has been presented it is perhaps evident that in sum the effect of the status system, though essential to coherence, coordination, and *esprit de corps*, is to reduce flexibility and adaptability. When the external conditions to which an organization must be adapted are stable, the importance of flexibility and adaptability is much less than under rapidly changing conditions, and the importance of coherence and refinement of coordination, in terms of efficiency, is much greater. Were it possible to forecast for a long period what the conditions will be, the problem in principle would be merely to establish an optimum system of status, a mean between extremes minimizing disadvantages and dangers, but reasonably conserving the advantages and certainly adequate to the minimum necessities. It would hardly be appropriate to call such a problem a dilemma. The dilemma lies in the fact that future conditions cannot be forecast correctly. Hence for current purposes it is necessary to employ and often to elaborate a system of status whose inherent tendency is to become unbalanced, rigid, and unjust.

We have seen that both functional and scalar systems of status are necessary to formal organizations of scalar type but that interests are generated by or within them forcing them to rigidity, lack of correspondence to real merits and real needs, and to hypertrophy, especially in their symbolic functions. As these matters are reflected on and as the technical apparatus of organization is studied, no doubt corrective measures can be known. They can be applied, however, only with great difficulty from within an organization, for even the chief executive is the chief of the status system and dependent on it. It therefore requires endless persistence, extraordinary ability, and great moral courage to control the dangerous developments in them. Probably, the principal needs can be summarized as three: to ensure that there is correspondence between status and ability by free movement; to prevent the systems of status from being ends or even primary means; and to see that the emoluments of office and of trade or profession are proportionate to the necessary level of incentives and morale. Some devices, *e.g.*, retirement rules, are known that facilitate these controls; but this is not the place to discuss them.

Insofar as we are concerned only with subordinate organizations, the correction of the pathologies of status systems in relatively "free" societies is largely accomplished by competition, regulation, and the pressure of public opinion, attended by the disintegration of organizations that cannot correct conditions. This does not usually involve catastrophic effects except for a few individuals, or sometimes for small communities. When the organization is that of a highly centralized state, however, it is doubtful whether there is as yet any means of correcting extreme investment of interests in the system of status, except by revolution or by military defeat.

Chapter V

THE MOTIVATION OF THE UNDER-PRIVILEGED WORKER

ALLISON DAVIS

IF YOU ask Mr. Turner, the boss, why Phil Moore is a hard and skillful worker, Mr. Turner will answer, "Because Phil comes from good stock." If you ask the boss why Henry Spears, the Okie "immigrant," does poor work, he will reply, "Because he comes from bad stock."

When the boss says "bad stock," he usually means "bad" heredity, *i.e.*, innate inferiority. The boss, himself, has not learned that cultural environment and training are the chief reasons for the differences between the work habits of Phil and Henry. Like the average teacher or parent, the boss believes almost religiously that "blood will tell." His exaggerated belief in the scope of heredity will be made even clearer if the visitor asks him what he thinks of Negro, or Mexican, or Italian-American workers.

"Not much," he says cynically. "But after all, what can you expect of them? They all come from lousy stock, you know."

The boss is raising, in the natural fashion in which it daily recurs, the problem of heredity and environment. In his case the burden of proof rests upon this honest and no doubt well-intentioned man. For, until workers from little Italy, Okietown, and the Black Belt can be given environments similar to those from the "respectable" neighborhoods (that

84

is to say, *equal chances* for developing their innate abilities), such workers cannot be judged scientifically, with regard to their comparative *hereditary* abilities. As Professor Jennings, the outstanding American geneticist, said in the *Biological Basis of Human Nature* more than a decade ago, ". . . bad living conditions often produce the same kind of results that bad genes do. Persons may become idle and worthless, insane, criminal, or tuberculous either through bad genes or through bad living conditions, or through a combination of both. So long as living conditions are bad we do not know what ills are due to bad genes."

The attitudes toward underprivileged groups, which I have described, are shared by most persons who have to train and supervise underprivileged workers in service and industry. As a rule, management has the attitudes, habits, and values of middle-class groups. Their attitudes toward, and standards for, work behavior are a part of their middle-class indoctrination. They are the result of the powerful motivation and the long processes of training, extending from early childhood through adult life, which the individual born into either the middle class or into the skilled working class receives in his family, in his social cliques, and in his social class.

The foreman's and the administrator's emphasis upon punctuality, responsibility, and the desire and drive to get ahead in life is part of their culture. They have *learned* all these traits. Not one of them has been inherited—through the foreman's or the vice-president's family, or his race, or his nationality. All these traits of the good worker, or good administrator, have had to be learned through training, family pressure, work opportunities, and through encouragement and reward on the job. To the foreman or the vice-president these traits and habits of his seem so integral to his behavior, so much a part of him, that he regards these virtues as entirely his *individual* achievement.

In fact, however, they are a part of his cultural environment, of the way of life, of the social environment with its social and economic rewards and punishments, in which he has been reared. They are part of a vast, overpowering group of social influences, of determinants of behavior, which have produced his own behavior and that of his family as well. His work habits, his ambition, his values, as well as the very disgust that he feels toward the habits of underprivileged workers, are chiefly the result of the family training, of the community standards and of the culture—the system of habits and attitudes—which he has learned.

Just as the members of the higher skilled working class and of management act in response to their culture, to their system of social and economic rewards, so do the underprivileged workers act in accord with their culture. The habits of "shiftlessness," "irresponsibility," lack of "ambition," absenteeism, and of quitting the job, which management usually regards as a result of the "innate" perversity of underprivileged white and Negro workers, are in fact *normal responses* that the worker has learned from his physical and social environment. These habits constitute a system of behavior and attitudes which are realistic and rational in *that environment* in which the individual of the slums has lived and in which he has been trained.

My purpose is to trace the origin of these work habits in the social and economic system of the communities in which the underprivileged worker has to live. I shall be specific and concrete. I shall not take time to indulge in sociological abstractions, but I shall try to deal with realities, with the habits of sleeping, of medical care, of joint communal living, of housing, of tavern and night-club life, of gambling, of sex, and of the social competition that the underprivileged worker learns from his slum environment.

The evidence will be taken from several studies of white and Negro working-class groups in the Chicago area, studies recently carried out by my colleagues and myself in The University of Chicago. They include evidence on 600 families, both white and Negro. Of these, 200 were middle class, and 400 were working class. In addition, the studies include intensive observation and interviewing of selected white and Negro working-class families in their homes, where they were observed several times a week throughout nearly a year. The intensive studies of Pearl, a white underprivileged worker, of Ruth, an even more underprivileged Negro worker, and of Clark, a lower class white worker, will be used to illustrate the findings of the statistical data on 600 families.

Pearl Elno, the white female worker, was born of old native stock in southern Indiana, the daughter of a coal miner. At the beginning of the great depression, her father came to Chicago to seek work, bringing his family. Here Pearl met Jim Elno, a young machinist, the son of a Polish laborer and a charwoman, and, like both his parents, extremely devoted to liquor in general and to schnapps in particular. At eighteen, Pearl married Jim Elno. Both youngsters were ambitious and smart. They were both good workers, anxious to buy a home of their own, and to get ahead in the world. Jim studied hard at his trade; and he bought a derby hat and a pair of spats—just to show his friends that he was a man who took himself seriously and intended to get somewhere in the world.

His young wife was always more practical and conscientious than Jim, and forced him to leave his mother's, set up a home of his own, and to work for goals more enduring than a derby and spats. All her efforts for a house of their own and for a decent standard of living were defeated, however, during the next 10 years, by the rapidly increasing number of their children. Jim was a Catholic, and Pearl was a very fertile woman. In 9 years, she bore seven children.

Unable to secure work during most of the thirties, and

presented annually with a new baby by Pearl, Jim began to drink heavily. Any father who has had to come home to five, or six, or seven small children, and has had to try to live and sleep with them, crowded into a three-room flat, will sympathize with Jim, I imagine. During the depression, four children were born to the Elnos. They had to flee to steadily smaller and poorer apartments, and the children were reduced to half-starvation rations, which kept them sorely undernourished and chronically ill. Unemployment and their hopelessly large family wore away the determination and the morale of the parents, especially of Jim. They separated twice, and Jim deserted once but returned. He was arrested two or three times for panhandling while drunk. He beat his wife several times, when he was drunk. The Elnos and their seven little children were on the rocks and seemed headed for the bottom.

But Pearl still had her own parental family. Her father and mother, and her sisters, together with their husbands, formed a closely organized and loyal clan, which repeatedly rescued her and her seven children. The sisters took them in, when Jim was violently drunk, or when they were evicted for inability to pay the rent. They bought the children clothes, and helped feed them. Pearl's mother, still able to hold a job at sixty, borrowed money on her home to lend to Jim, when he was employed by the Works Progress Administration. She came up from southern Indiana repeatedly to care for the children, so that Pearl could work as a waitress, and as a machine operator, to help feed the children while Jim was unemployed. One of Pearl's sisters opened a tavern recently and employed the mother, who in turn helped Pearl's family. Both the sisters and mother thus have continued to help Pearl.

The history of the Elno family illustrates in part how the organization, and the typical experiences of the white working-class family, control the motivation of the lower class worker. First, its size is typical of working-class families, and it is an important factor in their motivation. We found the average number of children in white *middle-class* families in Chicago to be only 2.2. In white working-class families, the average number of children is 3.3. This is a tremendous difference; along with the lower incomes that go with these much larger families, it changes the nature of family relationships in the working class, the methods of child training, the standards of nutrition, of cleanliness, of education, and of sex behavior. The actual daily pressure of 5 to 10 hungry stomachs to fill, backs to clothe, and feet to cover forces the working-class parent to reduce his ambitions to this level of subsistence; to lower his sights as far as long-term planning and studying for better jobs and for finer skills are concerned; to narrow, limit, and shorten his goals with regard to the care, nutrition, education, and careers of his children.

This terrible pressure for physical survival means that the *child* in the average working-class family usually does not learn the "ambition," the drive for high skills, and for educational achievement that the middle-class child learns in his family. The working-class individual usually does not learn to respond to these strong incentives and to seek these difficult goals, because they have been submerged in his family life by the daily battle for food, shelter, and for the preservation of the family. In this sense, ambition and the drive to attain the higher skills are a kind of luxury. They require a minimum *physical security;* only when one knows where his next week's or next month's food and shelter will come from, can he and his children afford to go in for the long-term education and training, the endless search for opportunities, and the tedious apple polishing that the attainment of higher skills and occupational status requires.

Secondly, the Elno family's history illustrates the deprivations, the shocks of fortune, the drain of illness and malnutrition, as well as the social and psychological disorganization, that reduce the efficiency of the underprivileged worker. A society that pens families into this kind of physical and social environment actually cripples both the ability and the work motivation of its workers. If there is one thing that modern psychology makes clear, it is this: men cannot be motivated successfully to work hard, or to learn well, simply by putting the screws upon them. The starvation theory of wages may or may not have been abandoned in actual industrial practice, but it is certain that other theories of social punishment, and of economic pressure, other theories that men will work hard and well *only* when they are *compelled* to by economic or legal necessity are still very popular. But the analysis of our system of economic and social prestige, as well as the findings of psychologists, make it clear to any realist that men work hard and learn well only when they have been trained to work for increasing rewards.

To improve the underprivileged worker's performance, one must help him to learn *to want* and to be anxious to attain higher social goals for himself and his children. All one can get out of methods of starvation conditions in wages, or of threat and intimidations, is more of the same inferior work and more concealed resistance, as in the case of a man whipping a poorly trained mule. The problem of changing the work habits and motivation of people who come out of families like the Elnos' is far more complex than mere supervision and pressure. It is a problem of changing the goals, the ambitions, and the level of cultural and occupational aspiration of the underprivileged worker.

This change in his cultural motivation cannot be attained by getting him into the starvation box. For, as the Elno family illustrates, the average working-class family is a large economic unit, a clan of kin. They can depend upon *each other* for shelter and food in time of unemployment, or of

90

reduced income, or of prolonged absenteeism, or when they simply quit the job. In this working-class culture, one may usually fall back upon his brothers, or sisters, or aunts, or nieces, or cousins for a bed and meals, in a way that middle-class people cannot. The middle-class adult person is ashamed to go to his relations or friends for food and shelter. "Respectability" prohibits such dependence. To avoid this embarrassing loss of "face," he will work harder, take more punishment of a mental and emotional kind on the job, and cling to the job more desperately than will the average lower class, underprivileged worker.

That is to say, the masses of working-class people, like the Elnos, cannot be frightened and forced into better work habits, simply through having the economic squeeze put on them, or through being threatened constantly with firing. Such threats do not intimidate them, as they do the middle-class clerk or schoolteacher, because the underprivileged worker is thoroughly accustomed to those conditions of life that middle-class people call "insecurity." Most important of all, he knows he can always "bunk in" with a relative, usually on his mother's side of the family, and he is certain that an extra plate will be filled for him and his, so long as his relatives have food. The harder the economic *noose* is drawn, the tighter the *protective* circle of the average working-class family is drawn. Thus economic intimidation is much less effective than with white-collar employees. Since most working-class people do not get the rewards of social and economic prestige in our society, they do not fear the loss of the job or the attendant loss of respectability in their communities nearly so deeply as do the white-collar workers.

One other example of this pattern of *group* economic help and solidarity should be included, before leaving the matter. In Negro families in the rural South, and generally in those which have migrated from the farms to Chicago, the circle of relations who help each other economically is even larger than in the average white working-class family. There are more children in these families; the average number of children in 300 Negro working-class families in the Chicago area is 4.9. The bonds of kinship, the closeness of feeling, and the number of mutual duties are also greater in the Negro working-class family, owing to its recent experiences as an integrated economic and social unit on the plantations.

There are also many broken white and Negro working-class families, of course. But these individuals, whose families have been scattered by death, disease, desertion, and immigration, are also provided with a communal group, which helps them in times of economic difficulty and illness. The life of Ruth, a Negro factory worker in Chicago, who was born in Mississippi, illustrates this point. Ruth's parents were unskilled workers, far below the Elnos in both education and opportunity for occupational training—at the very bottom of the economic hierarchy. The family came to Chicago in 1935. For a long time, they were unable to secure either work or relief. Both then, and later when the father was given a job as an unskilled laborer on WPA, Ruth, her four sisters and brother, and her parents lived in the large cellar of an old tenement on the South Side. The cellar had been divided into nine rooms, one for each family. There was no kitchen, only an open corner at the back of the cellar, with a small gas stove and a faucet. The nine families shared this corner as their "kitchen." But they had an organized, cooperative system of sharing, which went far beyond the joint use of the so-called "kitchen." They shared their small stocks of furniture, their bedclothes, and their wearing apparel. Most important of all, they shared their food and even their money. When a family was both out of work and off relief, the other families put their money and food into a communal "pot," in which the destitute family shared. This is a hard system to beat, for those who believe in the effectiveness of economic intimidation in making good workers. When workers can survive at this level, and still have the social support and approval of their friends, they can scarcely be threatened or starved into better work habits. They will have to be led, by the offering of concrete rewards of better job opportunities and wages and better treatment and status on the job.

In 1942, when Ruth was fifteen, her parents separated, and her mother remarried. This marriage forced Ruth out of her home at once. The next year she had to leave school and go to work. After she had to leave her home, but before she could obtain her working papers, Ruth lived, slept, and ate with the families of her working-class school friends. Often she had little sleep because there was no bed available, but she had a roof over her and at least a meal a day. She also shared the clothes of her school friends.

This communal, group living has persisted, even though Ruth has now been working for more than two years. She is a hard and powerful worker, who carries a man's load. Foremen pick her for heavy, driving jobs that not 1 woman out of 10 can stand. She likes to do this heavy work thoroughly, but she also finds it exhausting. Moreover, she is still very young, and she has no responsibilities except herself. Therefore, she stays off the job rather frequently and sometimes misses several days in succession. She can continue this habit, because she still has her group of friends, her large social clique, who are really her "adopted" family and who will give her shelter and food and lend her clothes whenever they have them. Therefore, Ruth disappears from the job even when she has *no* money. Keeping her broke, by paying her only every two weeks or every three weeks, will not keep her on the job. She can always "bunk in" with her group of friends. This is a typical experience of underprivileged workers, both male and female, and both in the South and in the North. Groups of people, who have *no families*, live together, share food, money, clothes, and beds,

93

and also share their work; for example, trading their ironing for another person's washing or cleaning.

It scarcely needs to be emphasized that this is a way of life that is demoralizing to the individual's habits of work. It is not realized generally, however, that the problem of increasing the efficiency of the underprivileged worker always involves two major kinds of difficulties that must be attacked. First his cultural goals must somehow be raised; his ceiling of aspiration for education, for respectability, for skills, and for better training of his children must become high enough to motivate him to work harder. Such efforts to change their cultural habits and their social status are the driving force behind those relatively few workers who do rise above the slum environments that I have been describing. Because this problem of motivating the lower class worker to strive hard for more respectable and complex ways of life is the more difficult problem, it will be considered last here.

The other, more immediate, more tangible task for our society in improving the efficiency of the labor supply is that of improving the underprivileged worker's standard of living. Workers who live under the conditions that I have described suffer heavy penalties in loss of sleep, malnutrition, and disease, which in turn greatly reduce their efficiency. Worst of all, from the point of view of those who wish to change these poor work habits, the slum dwellers become accustomed and "adjusted" to their crippling standards of living. Like people in every class, every culture, they learn to regard their environment and their living habits as decent and satisfying. This is the circle that our society must break, in order *to increase the consciousness of economic needs among the masses of workers,* and thus lead to fuller production and better labor.

The miserable housing, and recurrent homelessness of the underprivileged workers are the most costly of all drains upon his efficiency. A study of working-class Negroes in Chicago in 1944-1945 revealed that most of them had less than five hours' sleep per night. Children and adults must sleep three to five in a bed. Beds are usually filled day and night in Chicago's slums, as workers await their turn to sleep. The density of the population on the Negro South Side is the second highest in the United States.

Ruth sleeps in a kitchenette apartment rented by a mother with eight children. Ruth shares a bed with five other adolescents and children, sleeping crosswise the bed. She counts it a windfall when there are only three in the bed, and she may sleep lengthwise. A record of her hours of sleep was kept last winter, for two periods of two weeks each, one in November and one in January. She was in bed an average of 4½ hours out of each 24. During these 10 working days, she was absent 4. Her work was extremely heavy, so heavy that she was given a half hour's rest by the plant for each hour on the job. Without more sleep, she said, she could not stand the work even five days a week. She has been trying since Christmas to find a room to rent. Last fall she tried to find a kitchenette apartment, so that she could marry, but, as anyone who knows the South Side's residential "lock-in" understands, she had no chance.

Similar conditions prevail among white workers in many parts of the city, of course. In one large area restricted to whites on the South Side, the great majority of *families with children* live in single rooms, or in kitchenette apartments. No matter whether the people in these modern, urban rat-holes in which human children and their parents must live are white or Negro the social and economic results are the same. The children are forced out into the streets, day and night; they are "movie children" or completely vagrant children. Life cannot be lived as a family group in these packed rooms; it has to be lived on the streets, in the motion-picture theaters, the taverns, the bars, and the night clubs. Under such unimaginable living conditions, all the effort, training, and money, which in the case of the middle-class worker goes into his home, is blocked and diverted to sex, recreation, and gambling. How can a worker be motivated to work to furnish or to improve his home, when he cannot get an apartment, or even a bed to sleep in? The most basic goal, the most powerful organizing control in our society, or in any Western society, is the establishment and maintenance of a living place and a home. A society, such as ours, that deprives great masses of the workers of this primary goal, deprives them thereby of the prime incentive, the most insistent drive for steady, determined work habits. In addition, it directly reduces their efficiency on the job by the steady drain of exposure, lack of sleep, and the diseases, such as tuberculosis, which are related to overcrowding.

The physical disabilities of underprivileged workers in Chicago are far more extensive than the favorite publicity concerning their lack of orange juice and milk, and the occasional ratbites, would suggest. Unemployment and inadequate income resulting in chronic malnutrition decrease both their physical resistance and their working efficiency. A series of recent scientific studies of the children of underprivileged workers, as contrasted with children of middle-class parents have revealed that the vitamin and chemical levels in the blood of working-class children are greatly below those of middle-class children and are seriously deficient. A study of the bone structure of children in two such groups, by means of X ray, revealed that these nutritional and other environmental deprivations of working-class people leave their marks upon the very bones, themselves. In Chicago, the rates of infection and death from tuberculosis are far higher among underprivileged working-class groups, both white and Negro, than among middle-class groups, as revealed by a survey made at the University of Illinois. At the same time, hospital and medical care is far more limited and is critically limited for Negroes.

For the employer, the most important consideration here is that the underprivileged worker becomes accustomed to these conditions; he learns to accept poor habits of nutrition and medical care and to accept physical impairment as a natural part of his life. Ruth, for instance, eats only one meal a day, even when doing heavy labor. She has never been to a physician, or an optician, or an opthalmologist. Yet she is so nearsighted that she has to be within six inches of a newspaper or clock to read them; she is partly deaf from an early childhood accident, and she lived with a tubercular father for several years. But like Pearl, the white underprivileged worker, whose stamina is sufficient only for periods of a few weeks on a job, Ruth regards her physical impairment as "natural." She has not had the money nor the training requisite to secure good medical attention and to learn good health habits. Thus, both cultural attitudes toward nutrition and medical care, as well as severe limitations in housing and hospital facilities work together to reduce the efficiency of such workers. These social and economic drains accustom them to accept high absenteeism and chronic physical impairment as normal aspects of their work adjustment.

Education, as the underprivileged worker experiences it, likewise differs from the education of middle-class persons. It differs in its length, in its content, and in its value as a social and economic tool. In the Chicago area, the average number of grades completed by white *working-class* mothers is 8.6, whereas white middle-class mothers have completed an average of 14.2. White working-class fathers have finished the eighth (8.3) grade, on the average; by contrast, middle-class white fathers have completed an average of 16 grades. Among Negroes, the average for working-class parents is

even lower, but is rapidly overtaking that for white work-
ingmen.

On the whole, the Negro worker of the past generation in
Chicago—that is, those who are grandparents now—was
better educated than the white worker. Whereas 22.9 per
cent of our sample of white working-class women in that generation had no schooling at all, only 11.1 per cent of the
Negro working-class women had none. The proportion of
both white and Negro working-class women who had finished
grammar school was the same, 22 per cent. Among the
working-class men of this older generation, the Negroes were
nearly equal to the whites in years of schooling. Today, the
Negro lower class workingman is practically on a par with
the white worker with regard to grades completed in school.
For example, if we consider those who have spent some time
in high school, the proportion is higher among Negroes
(34.8 per cent as compared with 32.7 per cent). For instance, in our *middle-class* Chicago sample, both white and
Negro middle-class women had completed an average of 14
years in school. Negro middle-class men had completed 14.3
years, and white middle-class men 16.1 years. In the generation born since the First World War, moreover, Negroes
have greatly increased their average level of schooling. In
another decade, the Negro working class in the Chicago area
probably will have a higher average grade attainment than
the white working class. Their great handicap even now, in
the fifteen to twenty year age group is the lack of opportunities for apprenticeship, from which they are barred generally by both management and unions.

Among the present adult generations of underprivileged
workers, white or Negro, however, education has had little
effect upon work habits. Nor does it "take" very successfully with the slum child of any color.

Whereas, for the skilled worker and the office person both
their drive to work steadily and their interest in developing

their skills are powerfully stimulated by their training in school, for the average underprivileged worker, on the other hand, our schools are unrealistic in their methods and in their attempts at motivation. Furthermore, the schools are staffed by highly protected middle-class persons, whose goals and whose economic opportunities are quite different from those of the families and children of the lower class. To the underprivileged adolescent, the words and the goals of his teacher—those words and goals to which middle-class adolescents react with respect and hard striving—mean very little. For the words of the teacher are not connected with the *acts of training in his home*, with the actual rewards in school, or with actual steps in moving toward a career, which alone can make the words effective in motivating him to learn good school habits. Thus our educational system, which next to the family is the most effective agency in teaching good work habits to middle-class people, is largely ineffective and unrealistic with underprivileged groups. Education fails to motivate such workers because our schools and our society both lack *real rewards* to offer underprivileged groups. Neither lower class children nor adults will work hard in school or on the job just to please the teacher or boss. They are not going to learn to be ambitious, to be conscientious, and to study hard, as if school and work were a fine character-building game, which one plays just for the sake of playing. They can see, indeed, that those who work hard at school usually have families that *already* have the occupations, homes, and social acceptance that the school holds up as the rewards of education. The underprivileged workers can see also that the chances of their getting enough education to make their attainment of these rewards in the future at all probable is very slight. Since they can win the rewards of prestige and social acceptance in their own slum groups without much education, they do not take very seriously the motivation taught by the schools.

The impact upon the underprivileged worker of the physical and cultural environment that I have been describing is represented by the case of Clark, a twenty-four-year-old white man, who was intensively studied by an interviewer in the department of education. In 1939 and 1940, Clark was living in basement rooms, bunking in with friends. As conditions became too crowded even for that level of society, or as Clark wore out his welcome, he moved from one such refuge to another. He ate what he could buy with the change he made on odd jobs and what his friends could give him. Except for a meal from his friends two or three times a week he lived on two or three nickel frankfurters or hamburgers a day. For clothes, he had one frayed suit made of shoddy and a ragged half-cotton overcoat. He also had two pairs of trousers and two or three shirts, which he left for a time with various friends, and which were all eventually stolen.

In the fall of 1940, Clark went to work as a machine operator in a defense plant. He continued to bunk in with friends for several months. With the wages he earned the first three or four months, he bought chiefly food and clothes, paid his debts to his friends, and got drunk on week ends. As time went on, he spent about 75 per cent of his income on clothes, liquor, night clubs, and house parties. Less than a week after payday, he usually had to borrow his carfare to get to work, and to depend upon his friends for his meals, as well as for a place to sleep.

This behavior was part of a practical cultural system, however. His friends also depended upon him for loans and food, when *he* had just been paid. Thus, they actually had developed a system of getting money every Friday or Saturday, instead of only every second week, on payday. Each worker's payday was in reality a payday that he shared with one or two friends. Thus each man had a payday every

100

week. Their ideal was a payday every day, so that they would have ready cash always.

Like most of his group, Clark had a regular week-end bout of drunkenness and a series of parties. These lasted through Sunday night, so that he almost never went to work on Mondays. On other nights, he always stayed up until twelve or one o'clock. Since he had to be up by six in order to reach work on time, he averaged less than five hours per night, including week ends. He missed an average of 1½ days on the job, out of every week; sometimes because he did not have carfare or food; sometimes because his rest was too broken.

After about 15 months of work, Clark fell in love with a girl, and he began to take more interest in his job. He wanted to become a foreman, and began getting up at five o'clock in the morning, so as not to be late for work. He decided to marry the girl and for the first time began to "save" his wages, paying on furniture. He and the girl set out to find a place to live. Finally they discovered a tenement on the railroad tracks where the landlady agreed to rent them two rooms. They returned with their suitcases to discover that the landlady had decided she would rent only to men. In two months, they were unable to find any other place to live.

Clark is still living with his friends, four to a room, and has given up his plan to marry. He still spends almost all his wages on clothes, liquor, and recreation. He still misses at least three days on the job out of every two weeks. During the four years he has been working, however, there have been three periods when he improved his work habits, his punctuality, and his motivation. The first was when he wanted to marry, and actually was buying furniture, and looking for a home. The second period of improvement occurred later, when Clark was trying to become a foreman, in order to convince his girl's mother that he was not an "ignorant bum," as she claimed. The third period followed his first visit to a meeting of his union, and his resultant interest in winning status within the union. Each of these situations was a powerful stimulus to Clark's motivation on the job. From them, we can learn what makes him ambitious, and what can make him work more effectively.

First, however, what made him *fail* to work well? During these three periods when he actually wished to become an efficient worker and tried to change his habits, why did he gradually lose his drive and return to his old habits? The reasons seem clear enough. First, like Ruth, the colored worker, he was influenced powerfully by the fact that he had no home and was unable to find one. The effort of both these workers to find a home, so that they could marry, was blocked by our chaotic housing situation. A society in which a large proportion of the population cannot find a home—cannot even rent a home from the people who own them—is in this basic respect less well organized than most "primitive" societies. If people cannot find a place for themselves and for their families to live as a group, and to live fairly decently, according to their lights, their motivation to work hard is severely weakened. If the young adults cannot find a home, they usually cannot marry. Since marriage is one of the most powerful drives in motivating workers to accept responsibility and to "settle down," our housing situation is demoralizing to work habits.

Secondly, Clark failed in his hopeless desire to become a foreman, because both the habits he had learned and especially his lack of education made him unfit for this responsibility. He had gone only to the sixth grade, and he had not learned well what was taught in those grades. Like millions of underprivileged workers, he could barely write a sentence, even an ungrammatical sentence. Simple addition and subtraction were laborious problems for him. This educational handicap, plus the great mental and nervous strain created by the improvement of his habits (of his hours of going to bed and getting up, of his application to his work, of making time *every* day), is too great for 9 out of 10 individuals in his position to overcome.

Third, the same educational deficiencies and cultural habits, which prevented his improving his status in the plant, likewise made it impossible for him to attain any status in his union. The local, he found, was run by workers who were a step above him in social status, who were at the *top* level of lower class groups and sometimes were in the lower middle class. They had skills and habits with which he could not compete. He soon gave up this hope also, and thus his third powerful incentive to change his work habits was extinguished.

The most powerful of all the forces that keep him in his present way of life and of work are the pleasures that he actually can attain by following his underprivileged culture. He gets strong biological enjoyment. He spends a great deal of his nights in sexual exploration, since he does not have to go to work the next day. He lives in a social world where visceral, genital, and emotional gratification is far more available than it is in a middle-class world. Recreation, relaxation, and pure laziness from Friday night through Sunday night are extremely satisfying experiences. If such a week end leaves the worker too exhausted to get on the job Monday or even Tuesday and causes him to lose $10 or $15, it nevertheless is so organically rewarding that he will repeat the experience the following week end, or certainly the following payday.

Such are the emotional, the cultural, and the economic determinants of the work habits of the underprivileged worker. He lives in a different economic and social environment from that in which the skilled and the middle-class workers live. Therefore the behavior that he learns, the habits that are stimulated and maintained by his cultural group, are different also. The individuals of these different socioeconomic statuses and cultures are reacting to different realistic situations and psychological drives. Therefore their values and their social goals are different. Therefore, the behavior of the underprivileged worker, which the boss regards as "unsocialized" or "ignorant," or "lazy," or "unmotivated" is really behavior learned from the socioeconomic and cultural environments of these workers. In a realistic view, we must recognize it to be perfectly normal, a sensible response to the conditions of their lives.

If we wish to change these habits—and they are a great burden upon our production, because about one-third of our total population falls into this group—we must offer the underprivileged worker real rewards. They must be sufficiently powerful to repay him for the hard work and self-denial required to change his old habits, and to compete with the rewards of a physical kind that he already gets.

What are these real goals, for which he will work harder? The first is a place to live, a place that is not merely a kitchenette apartment, or a basement room, or a corner in a cellar, with three to six people to a bed. It has to be a place that appears desirable in the eyes of the underprivileged worker, a place he will "go for." Thus the first goal to be set before him, as a real, attainable probability is a permanent, decent home. This means a more permanent family life. This in turn means acceptance of responsibility and the setting up of long-term goals. And these require good, steady work.

A home, the rearing of a family, and the development of good work habits cannot be attained in a year or two. The underprivileged worker's goals are short term because his hold upon a job and upon clothes and upon food is short term. He knows well that he cannot establish a home, buy furniture, begin buying a house—all the endeavors that keep middle-class people busy and conscientious—in a year or two. He cannot educate his children, even through high school, on a few years of good wages. These basic social goals require a prospect of a steady job and good wages. This is what is meant by the words "economic and social security" to the middle-class person, namely, that there is an excellent chance that his work career and income will be steady and adequate to meet his standard of living. This is the kind of security possessed by middle-class people.

For the worker, short periods of good wages and plentiful jobs do not take the place of this security. One cannot change his way of living, or buy a home, or educate his children on this kind of income. To have a chance to develop stable habits of living, which means good work habits, people must have a stable job. The underprivileged worker is perfectly realistic when he asks, "Why should I try to save and get a little ahead in these times, when I'll be back on relief, anyhow, in a year or two?"

All this is to say that our society must offer the underprivileged worker a fair prospect, a better chance than he now has, of improving his status. It must convince him that he can secure a better life by hard work, and he can be convinced only when he *sees* a fair number of underprivileged *people like himself* getting reasonably secure jobs, a place to live, and a chance for promotion. I am *not* saying that society has to provide every such worker with permanent tenure and homeownership, and likewise make him a foreman, in order to motivate him to work harder. But I am saying that the underprivileged worker will not improve unless he finds that there is a chance of his getting the basic social and economic rewards that I have mentioned. He must be given the realistic hope that the game is worth the candle. If he *does change* his work habits, if he does become ambitious, if he does begin to crave respectability, then industry and society must have the homes and steady jobs and education to offer him in return for this great effort.

We see that middle-class people work like beavers and

have an insistent conscientiousness. They have the craving for respectability to drive them, and the hope of a better home, or better job, or higher status for their children to pull them. In order to make underprivileged people anxious to work harder and willing to bear more responsibility on the job, our industry, business, and government must convince them that they can get more out of life than they now get. This means that our system of production must expand so as to offer a larger proportion of the working class steadier jobs, good wages, and a decent place in which to live and to rear a family. Otherwise, a third or more of our white and Negro labor supply will become increasingly demoralized. In a society where even wars are won by the side with the largest skilled labor supply and the most efficient industrial structure, this is a vital consideration. In the future, our survival as a nation very likely will depend upon what happens to this one-third of our labor supply.

Chapter VI

RACE RELATIONS IN INDUSTRY

EVERETT CHERRINGTON HUGHES

O NE of the many dramas of modern industry is that of the meeting and of the working together of people unlike each other in race, nationality, and religion. Wherever it has gone—and industry is always moving into new parts of the world—it has put some new combination of the peoples of the earth at work together. The industrial revolution in England mixed the peoples of the South with those of the North and Irishmen with Englishmen. The Protestants of North Germany established industries in the Rhine; Catholic peasants of the region came to work in them. In the cotton mills of India, Hindus of various castes are herded together with their fellow Indians of other religions. Chinese city workers, driven from the urban East to the rural interior of their country by the Japanese invasion, even now find themselves making electrical equipment for war alongside rustics, also Chinese, who speak strange dialects and who until yesterday knew no tools more complicated than the sickle and the hammer.[1]

In our own country, immigrants from the back provinces of all the countries of Europe have met each other in the steel mill, the mine, the packing house and in the loft where ladies' handkerchiefs are made. Recently, they have been

[1] SHIH KUO-HENG, *China Enters the Machine Age,* Harvard University Press, Cambridge, 1944.

joined by a new wave of rural Americans, some of them as uninitiated to industry as any European peasant who ever landed on Ellis Island, but English of tongue, bred in the most indigenous American traditions of religion, folklore, humor, fighting and rugged individualism, and physically of the purest Anglo-Saxon stock, or of one of the combinations of African with Indian, Spanish, French, or Anglo-Saxon that we call "Negro" in this country.

Although each of the combinations of peoples thus brought together is unique, there is likeness in their meeting and its consequences. Wherever strange peoples have met to work in industry, some have been more initiated in its ways and have possessed more tools and technical knowledge than others. The new have always had to learn not merely how to use their hands and heads at new tasks but also how to live by a new calendar and by the clock, how to deal with new kinds of people in unaccustomed relations to each other, how to use money as their main source of income, and how to order their lives to a new set of contingencies. In nearly all cases, those older and better placed in industry have attributed the newcomers' lack of skill and of the industrial frame of mind to their inherent nature, without being too clear as to whether this nature is a matter of genes or of nurture. The newcomers sooner or later reorganize their ways and their wishes about the new order of things, and become aware of the opinions that their industrial superiors, both workers and employers, have of them. A difference of industrial status that they once accepted as in the nature of things they now question. They speak of discrimination. They act as self-conscious minorities, discontented with their status, always act. To compare these processes, as they have occurred in various places and with various human ingredients, is an intriguing enterprise. We leave it for another day, reminding ourselves only that the races, the nations, and the religions have met again and again in industry, that they will so meet again and again; that they can and do work together, although not always in harmony; and that the groups now oldest in industry learned their industrial lessons from ethnic strangers who considered them poor pupils until they became effective competitors or respected fellow workers. Thus do race relations in industry look in the world-wide, generations-long perspective.

Our special concern, however, is with the relations of Negroes with other persons in American industry at the present time. This requires other perspectives. For, while the Negroes are presently in a phase through which numerous other groups have passed, their situation in American life is unique. It is so in this respect, that the relations of Negro to white Americans have been crystallized into a body of practice enforced upon both races, but more especially upon the Negro, by social pressure, economic sanction, and even by physical force. White Americans have elaborated and then worked deep into their very bones a body of belief about what Negroes are and ought to be like, as well as a complex of fears of what would happen if the practices and beliefs were to change.

Beliefs and fears concerning the Negro as an economic being are interwoven with those concerning him as a citizen, neighbor, and companion. In white American thought, furthermore, strong belief that the Negro is different from other kinds of people is mixed in about equal proportions with fear that he is just like the rest of us. And here lies the essence of the race problem in America; we fear in the Negro those very human qualities that American social philosophy encourages in others. We stubbornly wish that the Negro should be unique. Race relations in American industry must be seen from this perspective also. The danger, however, is not that we should overlook the uniqueness of the relations between Negro and white Americans but that we should magnify it. We cannot avoid the race problem in

109

this country, although many people, especially in the North, would like to. All of us, Negro and white, are a part of the problem. It therefore behooves us to act as intelligently as possible. To do so, we must balance the unique features of the problem against its many likenesses with others. And we must see race relations in all the social matrices in which they occur.

One such matrix is industrial organization, considered as a system of human relations. And if I may present the conclusion of this chapter so near its beginning, that conclusion is not much more than the statement that "in industry" is the important term in the phrase, "race relations in industry." To know about race relations in industry, and to deal with them, one must look upon them as being of the same general order as other relations of people at work, requiring the same kinds of thinking and analysis, demanding the same understanding and skills; and, on the other hand, as little capable of settlement, once and for all, by some sleight-of-hand trick as other human problems in industry, and yet as amenable as others to those tentative, constantly repeated, never perfect, but often successful, decisions and actions by which a working organization is kept going to the moderate satisfaction of most people concerned.

The preceding chapters have presented a way of looking at industrial organization and at human behavior within it. Mr. Gardner gave us the important idea of an informal organization that can be discovered in each case only by close observation made with fundamental concepts in mind. Mr. Warner has shown how industry interacts with the community. Mr. Davis has talked of the life objectives that lead people to work and to have certain attitudes toward their jobs. Analysis of this kind may be applied to race relations in industry. Such analysis, stubbornly continued and applied to a variety of situations, will lead

110

to a better understanding not only of the race problem but also of industrial behavior in general. For what the introduction of a minority into an industry does is to throw into bold silhouette those very features of industrial organization and behavior with which these chapters have been concerned.

Perhaps the best answer to the question, "What is a minority in industry?" is this: if the hiring of persons of a certain kind in an industry, plant, or job is *news*, then that group is a minority. I refer, of course, not to the mild interest created by the coming into the shop of a strange individual or by the promotion of a person long known, but to the much more lively disturbance created by the hiring of workers of a strange category or by the promotion of individuals of a class hitherto limited to certain positions.

By this criterion, women and certain ethnic groups are minorities in industry. Negroes especially are a minority. For their appearance, like a good front-page story in the newspaper, furnishes the talking point for the day and not for the day alone. It causes people to talk, to listen, and to make dramatic gestures of alarm. Everyone recognizes that the decision behind the change is one of policy, very consciously made in the councils of management. The ensuing discussion will treat of the effects of the change on the labor market, postwar unemployment, seniority, and unions. But there will also be talk of things generally thought to be of less import and less related to what are claimed to be the main concerns of labor and management: such as washrooms, lockers, eating facilities, employees' sports and parties, including what to do about the shower to be held for the popular employee who is about to leave to have a baby. The people in the upper regions of management will be heard speculating upon the probable reactions of the humble janitress who will have to clean up washbasins used by the Negro employees. In short, the whole human side of the organization comes to life and to view. Relationships ordinarily unnoticed or even denied are consciously taken into account.

The emphasis upon informal relationships and what are ordinarily considered incidental matters appears not only at the moment when Negroes are introduced into a plant. Later on, managers, personnel men, and union officials attribute their success in integrating Negroes into their organizations to skillful manipulation not of the organization chart but of small groups and cliques and of the sentiments of the workers. A union official tells of setting the stage so that the hiring of Negroes may be defined as a victory for the union, thereby gaining support the members would otherwise have withheld. One company prides itself on having placed its first Negroes in the employment office for all to see, thus forestalling the criticism that the front-office staff was willing to give the shop hands Negro fellow workers but wouldn't have any themselves. Another placed a few on the periphery of a department where trouble was expected and let workers get used to having them around before moving them directly into the department. Others speak of handpicking their first Negro employees, not so much for their efficiency as to convince fellow workers that Negroes can be intelligent, good-looking, and "nice." Other employers, more jealous of their authority, and certainly not very pleased at the idea of hiring Negroes, admit that they did not succeed in getting the white workers to accept them. Indeed, the admission sometimes becomes almost a boast that hell, high water, and the Fair Employment Practices Committee combined couldn't make them do more than make a few defeatist gestures toward employing and promoting Negroes. Even this boastful admission contains the thought that success would require skillful handling of sentiments and the informal organization, rather than merely stronger use of the power to command.

These statements, and the legion of others like them, imply

112

not merely that the informal organization exists as a possible aid or hindrance to the hiring of minority workers, but that this organization is something that can be and sometimes is consciously manipulated. From the fact that such manipulation is possible people sometimes draw the unwarranted conclusion that the informal organization of workers and the sentiments expressed in their words and action are factors of little account. The facts point to the opposite conclusion, namely, that the manipulation is successful only to the extent that the informal organization and the sentiments of the workers are understood. To understand is not, however, to yield. All in all, it looks as if the greatest success in employing Negro workers has been achieved by a joining of understanding with firm and bold experimental action at the beginning and in the crises that arise later.

But how, in fact, do workers react to the coming of Negroes into their midst, and how does the informal organization operate. Let some examples speak. In a certain plant, Negroes were first hired in a department that, though dirty and smelly and without prestige, has a very stable working force. The men in it, mostly elderly Poles, work in groups of three that produce as units and are so paid as to make teamwork the key to a good income. It was thought that these men would not have much prejudice and that the isolation of the department would allow the hiring of Negroes without much comment. Of several Negro men hired, none stayed more than a few days. The management was disturbed, for it thought that the Negroes were confirming the common opinion that they are unreliable. Interviews with these Negro men brought out a consistent and simple story. The workers in the department had practiced every obvious and subtle art to let the newcomers know that they were not wanted and would never learn (*i.e.*, be taught) the work. Upon hearing all this an aged member of the management, now retired, snorted that no one had ever succeeded in 40 years in putting into that department any new man not chosen by the men already there. In this rather extreme case appear two factors: (1) the attitude of the men to the Negro newcomers, and (2) what we may call the molecular structure of their organization. We may leave the first with the remark that all the evidence in the case indicates that these men had no great prejudice toward Negroes as such, but that they had an ingrained suspicion of newcomers. On the second point, it is clear that formal admission to this shop meant nothing without informal admission to one of the work teams.

Now the organization of this particular shop was unusually close-grained. The power of each little work team to accept or reject a new worker was much greater than common. Instruction in the job was entirely in their hands. Another shop that we have examined is much more open. Each girl works on her own machine, so that her production does not mechanically depend upon that of another. In this situation it is hard to see how the older girls could prevent the new one from making her quota, and there is no reason to believe that they try. But it is a rare job that is not learned more quickly and satisfactorily if one gets pointers from fellow workers. It is doubtful whether any job, no matter how well organized the formal instruction for it may be, is learned entirely without such aid. The diaries of our fieldworkers are full of this theme. Of course, the instruction given the new worker is not confined to pointers on bettering his production; it includes devices for resisting pressure from management and the workers' own rules for dealing with one another. In fact, what the new worker gets—or does not get—from his fellows is an initiation rather than mere instruction. While he is being initiated, he is also being tried out to see what sort of fellow worker he will be. The place he is to have in the organization is being determined at the same time. What his job will mean to him

114

will depend, in a degree that varies with his personality and objectives, on this place. His performance as well will probably depend upon it. Elton Mayo and his associates have recently found that, in an aircraft plant on the West Coast, absences and turnover are much less frequent among men who are members of a work team with some group solidarity.[1]

Our findings suggest that Negroes are not generally initiated into existing teams and cliques of white workers. Occasionally we learn of such cases as that of a white group leader of southern extraction, who, being anxious to keep a good gang together in an unstable shipyard and finding that a Negro welder was a good and agreeable worker, invites the Negro to eat with the white group in order to be sure of keeping him. Individual Negroes are sometimes accepted as good fellows, although the price may be that they allow themselves to be considered exceptions, different from and superior to the common run of Negroes; a definition intended to be flattering to the individual, but derogatory of Negroes as a group. Sometimes, the initiation of the Negro includes a trying out of horseplay and nicknames on him, putting him in the dilemma of accepting the role of a comic inferior or of resisting and perhaps finding that the price of equality is isolation. Our files contain the statements of many Negro men who prefer to walk and work in lonely dignity; of others who become sensitive and aggressive; and of a few who by a combination of wit and good humor achieve both respect and friendship.

In a few plants that we have been able to analyze in some detail, however, such informal groupings of Negroes as exist are somewhat separate from white groupings. It seems plausible and, from the data, likely that informal organiza-

[1] Mayo, Elton, and George F. F. Lombard, *Teamwork and Turnover in the Aircraft Industry of Southern California,* Harvard University Graduate School of Business Administration, Boston, 1944.

tion has not developed so far among Negro workers in plants where they are new as among white workers. In a plant now being observed the Negro women in one department show signs of elaborating a system of cliques, with leaders who are not those whom the supervisors consider to be leaders.

While our data on this point are far short of what they should be, they indicate, as would our other knowledge of industrial behavior, that the formation of cliques, work teams, and leaders has and will have the same effect upon Negro workers as upon workers generally. It may be assumed that if there are to be leaders among Negro workers, they will arise only when there is something for them to lead, namely, cliques, work teams, and the like. It therefore becomes important to know what relations grow up or can be brought about between Negro groups and Negro leaders and their white counterparts. A significant lead on this problem lies in what appears to be true in certain racially mixed unions: that the knitting of the organization of the two races occurs not so much in the washroom and lunchroom gossip groups—the primary level of contact and interaction—but a little higher, at the level of minor leadership, where the enthusiasm for a common cause and the necessities of strategy favor a solidarity that transcends the race line.

An ulterior motive has led me to put off consideration of what is usually the main theme of discussions of race relations—what the races think and feel about each other. I wished first to direct your attention to the setting within which people's thoughts and sentiments are put into gesture and action. What, then, is the Negro in the minds of the white people who make industry's policies and put them into effect, of those lower supervisors whose identification with management has lately become a matter of dispute, of union leaders, and of workers? Again we shall emphasize general points rather than to give a detailed survey.

The American industrial executive prides himself on two

things pertinent to our subject. First, on his progressive, scientific attitude toward industrial processes. He wants new things done, but he wants them to be tested; boldness, with enough caution not to go wrong, is his formula. His second point of pride is his ability to choose men. He is proud of the "comers" he has picked out and given their chance. But Herman Feldman, who made a survey of racial factors in American industry about 15 years ago, found that, while nearly all employers had positive opinions about the characteristics of various nationalities and races as workers, they had little or no systematic evidence on the subject. "Actual analysis," he said, "of the comparative capacity of different racial groups is not part of the practice of industrial concerns." [1] Our own evidence confirms the impression that the view of most industrial managers is clouded by the brand names of race and nationality in about the same measure as that of other people. On a number of occasions I have been asked to discuss race relations in industry with groups of industrial men in managerial posts from the very modest, but promising, to the highest. Invariably I have been asked to talk about the matter in a practical way; *i.e.*, to stick to the experience that industries have had in adjusting the relations of Negro and white workers. After complying with this request I have always been showered with questions. Of the questions asked by these practical men, the great majority have been questions about the Negro, not race relations in industry; *i.e.*, not about the kinds of situations that arise when Negroes of certain kinds and in certain proportions work with non-Negroes of certain kinds and in certain proportions under different circumstances. The questions, furthermore, have been affirmative in mood, beginning with an "Is it not true that Negroes . . . ?" or "When will Negroes learn . . . ?"

[1] FELDMAN, HERMAN, *Racial Factors in American Industry,* p. 192, Harper & Brothers, New York, 1931.

The affirmations ill-concealed in these questions had not to do so much with the Negro's aptitudes for learning manual and mental skills, as with his social nature. Taken together, they express the American stereotype of the Negro, a creature unfit for any but the marginal positions in industry because of his laziness, primitiveness, and childlikeness, yet full of an unjustified desire to have what he does not have and should not want to have, up to and including marriage with the manager's secretary. Let me hasten to assure you that these questions were usually answered by other members of the same groups, less numerous, but keenly interested in reporting their own experience and in learning from the experiences of others. The fact that the bulk of these men of managerial rank think of race relations in much the same way as other Americans does not prove that they are incompetent managers, or that many of them have not very successfully hired Negroes to work alongside their white workers. Many of them have done so.

The fact that many people in managerial positions so think of the Negro is, however, significant. It means that the decision to hire Negroes at all where they have not been employed before, or to hire them for new kinds of jobs is generally regarded as a step into a dangerous unknown. It indicates that the natural and normal thing is not to employ Negroes, and that to employ them or to extend their employment to new fields, to skilled work, or to the office, has the weight of sentiment and precedent against it.

Another consequence of this kind of thinking is a strong disposition to regard the employment of Negroes as a very tentative experiment, something to do only in an emergency. There are two extremes of the experimental frame of mind. One is that stubborn and determined attitude that makes the experimenter look closely for the causes of any apparent failures. His disposition is to retain faith in his experiment and to seek the causes of failure in the manner of applica-

118

tion rather than in the idea itself. The other frame of mind is that of trying, timorously and tentatively, against one's own conviction, some unfortunately necessary departure from routine. In this frame of mind, that of many representatives of management toward the hiring of Negroes, one is sensitive to the objections of others in his own organization, touchy about the "I told you so" that perhaps accords with his own feelings. This frame of mind is revealed in the inclination of many managements to see a racial issue in any difficulty in which Negroes are involved. This tendency is of course given strength by a like tendency of employees, both Negro and white. In a typical case of this kind the management frantically called the representative of an agency that tries to settle such matters to say they were having race trouble and would have to establish separate locker rooms. The investigator found that the plant had grown tremendously during the war, without any increase in locker-room facilities. For two years employees had been complaining of crowding in the locker room and of having to share their lockers with workers on other shifts. When Negroes were hired, the matter came to a head; the white employees demanded separate locker rooms. This case was settled by immediately building new but not segregated locker rooms well placed about the plant. The racial way of thinking in this case gave a ready definition for a chronic problem.

Such a timorous and tentative attitude cannot but influence the already unfavorable views of workers and lower supervisors toward Negro workers and encourage their resistance. One cannot expect people to change a satisfying and socially supported attitude unless there is some counter-satisfaction or support. Workers, like other people, look for rewards. They talk and act to the gallery more than they are given credit for. Management, by and large, has not thought much of how to reward and support the employee in a change of attitude toward strange ethnic groups and Negroes. The lower supervisors do not generally do so. Fellow workers certainly are more inclined to reward a person for thinking and acting in the conventional way toward Negroes. Unions act sometimes one way and sometimes another; there is a great difference between them in this regard.

To turn more directly to the attitudes of workers, the diaries of observers in industry indicate a certain rewarding of the dramatic, unqualified, rather than of the moderate statement of attitudes. A worker may be taken down a peg if he boasts about how he talked back to the boss, not because of the attitude expressed, but because he is suspected of not having done it in the way he said. When a company says it will hire Negroes, if people don't mind, some of their people say they will quit. They are needled afterward, not for the threat, but for the failure to carry it out. We have found no case, except in some of the unions that have set about to alter racial attitudes, in which either fellow workers or supervision give the individual worker any efficacious reward for expressing a favorable attitude toward Negroes.

If we look at the structure of the thinking of workers about Negro fellow workers, we will find in it not merely the conventional American attitude toward Negroes, but also the general inclination of workers to view with disapproval, born of anxiety, the hiring of new kinds of workers for their particular jobs. Their anxiety relates not only to security but to status and prestige as well. Jobs and departments in an industry are rated by everyone concerned. We expect that. Less attention has been given to the fact that the kinds of people hired for a given job determine to some extent the job's prestige. Thus, if women are hired for a job that only men have done, the men may take the hiring of women, not as proof that women are rising in status, but as proof that the job's status is threatened. We have heard of one industry in which Italians, who had been limited to poorer jobs, were annoyed when Negroes were hired to work alongside them; not because they disliked Negroes particularly, but on the ground that—since they knew what people thought of Negroes—the hiring of them was additional evidence that management had a low opinion of the Italians. Like most other actions of management, the hiring of new kinds of workers is regarded as a social gesture, as an expression of management's opinion of the job and of the people already on the job. It also changes the situation of the workers, in that they have to size up and judge how the new, unknown people will act toward the work group, the union, and management. Much talk is required among the workers to arrive at new common understandings about how to behave. The disposition of the workers is, at the beginning, to resist changes in the composition of their work group, and to give the rewards to those who crystallize the unfavorable opinion rather than to those who explore the situation for favorable aspects and interpretations.

On the other hand, while workers do not like the prospect of new kinds of fellow workers, they have a disposition to "go along" with most people hired. An American girl of Polish descent spoke for thousands of workers in northern cities when she said of Negroes, "I'd rather not work with them myself, but I wouldn't quit because of them. I guess they have to work somewhere, but I wish it didn't have to be here." A good many white workers report that, in their place of work, there is an "exceptional" Negro, who is a good worker, doesn't try to "mix too much," and who himself is the first to assert that most Negroes aren't much good. Others speak of a Negro who is an effective shop steward or member of a grievance committee. Still others report that the Negro girls in their shop are clean, agreeable, or of a good class. These reactions indicate that racial stereotypes, even though believed in, are to some extent seen for what they are and are not always applied to individuals whom one knows well enough to define in terms of the qualities considered desirable in fellow workers.

We have said but little about the protagonist of race relations in American industry, the Negro industrial worker. As a matter of fact, in our research we have learned more from him than from any other source and more about him—and her—than about anyone else. Being a self-conscious member of a minority, he knows more and will tell more about the problem than white workers. What is to others a passing incident is to him his fate. He is clearly of one of the most rapidly changing groups in the country; his skills and experience are being transformed. His hopes and demands, no less so. And if one reads through the hundreds of interviews in which Negro workers tell us the story of their experiences in industry, he will see laid before him all that variety of life objectives by which Americans gauge the worth and meaning of their jobs. The main difference is the preoccupation of all Negroes—each in a way that reflects his backgrounds, his conception of himself, and his views of the realities of the American world in which he has to live—with the race problem.

These observations concerning American workers who are Negroes give an easy excuse for ending this chapter, like a good sermon, where it began. The differences among Negroes in the qualities pertinent to their behavior as workers and fellow workers are significant only to those people—employers, union leaders, and workers—who are in that stubbornly experimental frame of mind of which we spoke; the frame of mind in which one applies to the problem of race relations all that we know and can learn about human relations in industry.

Chapter VII

WHEN WORKERS AND CUSTOMERS MEET

WE HAVE been looking at the factory as a social system, but we must recognize the fact that the factory is not the only kind of social system to be found in American industry. There are other types of structures, and, as the structures differ, so do the human problems that are experienced in those organizations.

When workers and customers meet, in the service industries, that relationship adds a new dimension to the pattern of human relations in industry. When the customer takes an active part in business activity, the whole organization must be adjusted to his behavior.

While all service industries have the customer relationship in common, there are nevertheless important structural differences among industries in this group. For example, the restaurant industry differs from the others in certain respects that make it particularly interesting for human relations research.[1]

The restaurant is a combination production and service unit. In this it differs from the factory, which is solely a production or processing unit, and it also differs from the department store, which is solely a service unit.

[1] The National Restaurant Association sponsored the research on which this chapter is based. However, the views expressed are the sole responsibility of the author.

The restaurant deals in a perishable commodity, which can be produced only a little in advance of its consumption, and it must serve customers whose numbers can never be exactly foreseen. If the food estimates prove to be low, then the kitchen runs out of a number of popular items, and there are delays in providing new orders or substitutions. This upsets the customers, who in turn upset the waiters or waitresses, and so on until the pressure is carried right into the kitchen. On the other hand, if the food estimates prove to be too high, then food is wasted, costs go up, and the restaurant loses money. Consequently the restaurant always faces a difficult problem of coordination of production and service departments—a problem, which, so far as I know, is to be found in no other industry.

The human relations problem faced by the worker is also quite unique. Nearly every restaurant worker must adjust to people in at least two different relationships—in addition to getting along with fellow workers on his own job. For example, the cook responds to the directions of the kitchen supervisor and also must respond to requests for food from kitchen runners or supply men. Similarly, the pantry worker is under the pantry supervisor and responds to orders for food from waitresses. For the waitress, the problem is a good deal more complex. She must adjust herself to supervisor and to other waitresses and in addition she has to deal with between 50 and 100 customers a day, many of them complete strangers; and she has to adjust to service pantry workers or cooks to get the food out, and to bartenders to get her drinks, if the restaurant serves liquor. Clearly it requires a high degree of social adaptability to handle this assignment successfully.

As far as the workers are concerned, the factory is characterized by a predominantly straight line authority. The restaurant has that straight line but, in addition, it has what we might call a diagonal line of action extending

124

from customer straight through to dishwasher (see Fig. 3 below).

We might expect this situation to give rise to special problems of adjustment, and that is indeed what we have found.

THE RESTAURANT
(SIMPLIFIED DIAGRAM)

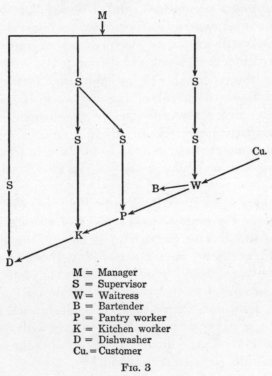

M = Manager
S = Supervisor
W = Waitress
B = Bartender
P = Pantry worker
K = Kitchen worker
D = Dishwasher
Cu. = Customer

Fɪɢ. 3

However, before we explore these problems, it should be pointed out that only a part of the behavior we observed in our restaurant study could be attributed to the distinctive structure of the restaurant itself. Our research was carried on during the war when restaurant people were working under the "abnormal" pressures of wartime. However, in some respects this is an advantage, for much of our knowledge of normal individuals is derived from the study of abnormal psychology. Similarly, we can expect to increase our understanding of human reactions to the ordinary tensions of everyday life through observing the breakdowns that occur under abnormal pressure.

Faced with acute food shortages, additional work to meet new government regulations, and with a labor force short in numbers and experience, restaurant organizations faced extraordinary difficulties in meeting their record volume of consumer demand. To one who has seen the industry from the inside, the remarkable thing is not that there were frictions and tensions but rather that restaurants managed to function so well under such severe handicaps. However, there were extra pressures, and there were some people who broke down under pressure. It is to these individuals and to the high-tension situations they faced that I will give my attention.

Since there is not space to consider the whole organization, let us look at the problem at the point of customer contact, where the waitress meets the customers. (To simplify the story, waiters will not be considered here, though their problems are quite similar.) That raises several questions. How do waitresses react to customers? How do customers react to them? How does the customer relationship affect the behavior of the waiter or waitress in contacts with supervisors or other workers? And finally, what role does the supervisor play in handling customer relations?

To answer these questions, I shall give special attention to the crying waitress. Of course, it should be understood that even under wartime pressure only a small minority of waitresses were subject to crying spells. However, crying is worth attention because it furnishes quite an objective manifestation of behavior. As we explore that, we can ask what situations give rise to crying and then ask further which waitresses cry and which do not. As we answer those

questions, we shall be able to draw conclusions upon the
nature of the human relations situation and also upon the
relationship between the social background and social ties
of the waitress and her behavior under pressure.

What nervous tension means to the waitress can hardly be
explained in general terms. We must go to the girls themselves to get that story. Here is an example that brings out
most of the elements common to the crying situation. The
waitress in this case is a girl of about twenty-one, with a year
of experience in a large and busy Loop restaurant. She put
it this way:

You know, I was so mad! I finally broke down Tuesday and
cried. That was really a terrible day. The guests were crabby,
and I wasn't making any money, and we kept running out of
food in the kitchen.

Once I went past one of my tables just when a new party was
sitting down. One of the women picks up 50 cents and puts
it in her pocket. She says, "Look, the people here must have
forgot and left their money." I could have screamed, but what
could I do?

Well the guests were yelling at me all day, trying to get my
attention. Everybody had trouble. Sue cried too.

The waitress was asked if she could remember the particular incident that set the crying off.

Yes, it was like this. I was rushed, and I came in to the
service pantry to get my hot plates. There were three hot
plates standing up there on the counter, and, when I called my
order in, the woman standing behind the counter just said,
"Take them," so I put them on my tray and started out. I
thought I was doing all right, but then Sue comes in. You see
she had been stuck all day. She had orders for hot plates for
her whole station all at once, and she couldn't carry it all out,
so she left some of her hot plates at the counter and told the
woman behind the counter to save them for her.

When she came back and saw the hot plates all gone with a

long line of girls waiting to get them, she started to cry. Well, when I saw that the plates were really hers, I gave them right back to her, and a couple of other girls gave plates back to her, so she got her hot plates right back, and she didn't have to leave the floor.

But that upset me. You know, I was getting out of a hole with those hot plates, but then all of a sudden I had to give them up and get right at the end of a long line. I just started to bawl.

I had to go down to the rest room. Well, the way I am, I'm just getting over it when I think again what one of the guests said and the way they were acting, and then I get feeling sorry for myself some more, and I start to cry all over again. It took me an hour to get back on the floor Tuesday.

Here we see that there is no one cause for crying. Rather it is a combination of pressures. This was a bad day in the coordination of production and service. The food was not ready when the waitreses needed it, and, when it did come up, there was a failure of adjustment between waitresses and counter people. Related to this problem, a number of the girls were having trouble in getting along with their customers.

The waitress brought up one important aspect of the customer relations problem: the matter of tipping. Her experience with customers pocketing the tip left by their predecessors was unusual. Her comment that on this particular bad day she was not making any money was a remark that we heard all the time. Even in high-quality restaurants there are always a certain number of "stiffs"—customers who don't tip.

Since it is well known that the waitress's income depends upon tips more than wages, we might be tempted to put down the "stiff" as an economic problem. However, when we get the girls to talk about the situation, it is clear that this is not the case. We asked one girl to explain how she felt when she was "stiffed." She said,

You think of all the work you've done and how you've tried to please those people, and it hurts when they don't leave anything for you. You think, so that's what they really think of me. . . . It's like an insult.

A restaurant owner told me that in a place he operated where "stiffing" was quite rare, he would find one of his best waitresses in tears from time to time. She would always explain, "I failed, Mr. Blank, I failed today. After all I did for them, they didn't like me."

Waitresses, like other people, are conditioned by their experiences in growing up to expect recognition when they are of service to someone. The recognition need not necessarily be a material reward, but it is the custom, under the tipping system, to put it in that form. Consequently, the waitress can't help feeling a sense of personal failure and public censure when she is "stiffed." She may try to look at the situation rationally, saying that some people just never tip, or perhaps they just forgot it, or they may not have had the right change, and so on, but this does not alter the fact that her expectations were frustrated.

The relationship between expectations and events is clearly an important one. Factory studies have shown that the development of certain routines in handling the job and a certain pattern of adjustment to fellow workers and supervisors help to give the worker emotional stability and a sense of satisfaction. The restaurant job and its human relations can never be fitted into a pattern of routine. The experienced waitress develops certain skills in organizing her work so as to keep her various customers occupied and get the food out of the service pantry, but these skills must be continually put to the test in meeting changing conditions in the dining room and in the service pantry. There are always new problems to be solved. And—perhaps most unsettling of all—there are the solved problems that suddenly become unsolved, as in the case of this waitress who thought she was getting out of a hole, only to find herself more deeply involved than ever.

The waitress in this case says that she could have screamed. If she had screamed, probably she would not have had to cry. The relationship is well recognized by the waitresses themselves. As one of them said,

> The trouble is, when the guests get nasty with you, you can't tell them off. You have to keep it all inside you. That's what makes it so nerve-racking. It would be much easier for us if we could talk back.

It is clear that the pressures upon the waitress cannot simply be absorbed. In one way or another, they must come out, and crying is one outlet.

The waitress who told us this story was talking about "one of those days" when everything seems to go wrong. There are days when everything seems to run along fairly smoothly, and then there are days when something goes wrong at the start and everybody is under great pressure all day long. Tension and confusion, when once under way, tend to build up and reinforce each other. If the waitress once gets upset in her relations with her customers, she is likely to have trouble all day.

This was clearly shown in one restaurant we studied. There the difficult customers seemed to run in series. We often heard the girls comment, as they finished work, "What a night! Just one of them after another." We have no statistics on the percentage of unpleasant to total customers from one night to another, but the wide fluctuations in the waitress's feelings towards customers certainly do not refer just to the personalities of the customers. She is reacting to a relationship. Whenever a difficult incident arises to upset this relationship, the waitress is thrown off balance and is more likely to get into difficulties with her next customers, so that social equilibirum may readily be destroyed for the whole working period.

The background gives us an idea of the situation in which crying takes place, but it must be noted that waitresses react to these tensions in varying ways. Some cry fairly frequently, some seldom cry, and there are some who never cry. If we are to understand this behavior, such differences must be explained.

The broadest generalization we can make is that crying behavior is related to length of waitress work experience. There are a number of reasons why this should be so. In the first place, there is a selective process at work, with girls who break down under the strain tending to drop out of the industry. The more experienced girls have more skill in organizing their work and have had practice in coping with almost any problem that may arise. Furthermore, in some restaurants where stations are assigned on a seniority basis, the more experienced girls tend to work in the same general location, where they are able to help each other. Inexperienced girls may be concentrated together too, but they generally have their hands so full with their own work that they can't provide each other with the help over rough spots, which is so important when the pressure is on.

As a rule, the more experienced girls are much more aggressive toward service pantry workers and bartenders, so that they are able to get some of the pressure off in that direction.

There are also important differences in relations with customers and with supervisors. Most experienced waitresses build up a following of steady customers. Sometimes the relationship becomes a very cordial one, and the appearance of a steady customer may completely change the situation for a waitress who has been in difficulty with strangers.

131

Even when the steady customer is an unpopular one, at least he is not an unknown quantity, and the waitress knows what to expect from him.

Experienced waitresses have generally made their adjustment to the standards of the restaurant and do not make many mistakes in their work. They are thus much less subject to criticism and enforcement of rules from supervisors. In fact, where we have observed it, the comparison is quite striking. The experienced waitresses proceed with little if any regulation of their behavior by supervisors, whereas inexperienced girls tend to be subjected to a good deal more attention from the supervision.

The matter of experience accounts for a great deal, but it does not tell the whole story. We find among inexperienced waitresses some who never cry and among experienced waitresses some who break down fairly frequently. If we look into these deviations from the expected behavior, and if we give close attention to several other cases where the factor of experience is held constant, then we should be able to come to grips with the dynamics of this crying behavior.

The first point that stands out is that the waitress who bears up under pressure does not simply respond to her customers. She acts with some skill to control their behavior. The first question to ask when we look at the customer relationship is, "Does the waitress get the jump on the customer, or does the customer get the jump on the waitress?" The skilled waitress realizes the crucial nature of this question. One of them gave these instructions to a new girl:

Get a clean cover on the table, give them their water, take the order, and then leave them if necessary. Once they have a feeling that you have taken charge, they will be all right.

The skilled waitress tackles the customers with confidence and without hesitation. For example, she may find that a new customer has seated himself before she could clear off

132

the dirty dishes and change the cloth. He is now leaning on the table, studying the menu. She greets him, says, "May I change the cover, please?" and, without waiting for an answer, takes his menu away from him so that he moves back from the table, and she goes about her work. The relationship is handled politely but firmly, and there is never any question as to who is in charge. Most customers react favorably to this approach. While we have not interviewed them on the subject, it appears that it gives them a feeling of security when the waitress moves right in and shows that she knows how to handle her work.

Getting the jump on customers involves not only such concrete moves as changing the tablecloth. It also involves giving the proper emotional tone to the relationship. This is a difficult matter on which to present objective data, but skilled waitresses know what they are doing and explain it along these lines:

The trouble with a lot of girls is that they're afraid of the guests. They wouldn't admit it, but they really are. You know, if you're timid, the guests can sense that, and I guess it's just human nature that people like to pick on you when you're timid. That way you get off on the wrong foot from the beginning, and you never get things right all day. I know how it is because I used to be afraid of people when I first started and I cried a few times the first month or two. But I've got more confidence now. I know there isn't any situation I can't handle.

A lot depends upon the way you approach the guest. I can tell it myself. If you go up to them as though you are afraid of them or as though you don't want to wait on them at all, they can sense that, and it makes them nervous and fussy. So I always go up to a guest as if I was happy to wait on the person. I try to make them feel comfortable and at ease to start with, and then I don't have any trouble.

133

While we need not accept the waitress's observation upon human nature, we can observe the behavior she describes. Apparently it is up to the waitress to seize the initiative in customer relations—to set the pattern for the relationship. This she does by the things she does, the things she says, the way she uses her voice, and the expression on her face. If she fails to seize the initiative in this manner, the customer senses her uncertainty and seems to feel uneasy himself. This is likely to lead to trouble.

However, the generalization needs this qualification. We can observe three general types of waitress-customer relationships. In one, the waitress holds the initiative from beginning to end. In another, the customer holds the initiative throughout. In the third, it is uncertain who is taking the lead and the initiative passes back and forth or remains in dispute. From the standpoint of the emotional stability of the waitress, either of the first two relationships is feasible, provided that the customer who takes the initiative frames his demands in a manner that will not bring the waitress into conflict with other employees and supervisors. It is the third type of relationship that seems to be the troublesome one, and this, incidentally, is most often a problem of the woman customer. The customer does not know what she wants yet refuses to accept the waitress's suggestions. She is not ready to give her order when the waitress wants to take it, and she wants to give her order when the waitress is occupied with other duties. And then she changes her mind. She does not want coffee with her main course, but when that course arrives she wants coffee after all. She will have the broiled scrod, but when her friend's chicken salad arrives it looks so good that she will have that instead. Such a relationship leads to a good deal of fencing between waitress and customer, and forces the waitress to reorganize her plan of work with every move the customer makes. It also gets the girl in trouble in the service pantry, as the employees there do not like to change orders. Such a customer therefore gives rise to a number of particular problems, but beyond that the basic difficulty seems to be that the waitress does not know where she stands and does not know what to expect.

While the waitress may get along well with the customer who seizes and maintains the initiative, that alone will not solve her problems. She must be able to lead those who want to be led and to get the jump on the uncertain and recalcitrant customers. She will always have difficult customers to deal with, but, with this approach, she will find that there are not enough of them to upset her equilibrium.

This would lead us to expect that girls with some leadership experience—with some experience in taking the initiative in human relations—would make the best adjustment to waitress work. We found that this did prove to be an important factor.

In one of the restaurants studied, we were fortunate in finding two sets of twins. In both cases, one of the pair broke down on the job fairly often, while the other never or hardly ever cried. Being able to hold the age and experience factors constant, and taking the girls from the same general family and community environment, we should be able to explore individual differences in patterns of interaction.

The Swansons, Ruth and Sally, were identical twins, and both said that they had always been "very close," doing nearly everything together. While both girls were considered shy and quiet, we found in interviewing them that Sally was decidedly more articulate. We drew Sally out on their relationship, asking how they decided what they were going to do. "Well," she said, "sometimes we would have arguments about it, but we would always decide to do the same thing in the end." We asked who usually won out in the arguments. She smiled and said, "I guess I usually did." We asked for an example of the sort of arguments they had. She said,

Well, lots of times it would be about clothes. Ruth would want to wear one dress, and I'd want to wear another dress. We'd argue it out, and she would finally wear the dress I wanted her to wear.

Ruth was the girl who cried. Sally never cried.

The Careys, Rita and Lucille, were not identical. Both were quite attractive, talkative, and popular with the other waitresses, but in the matter of social initiative, there were striking differences. This may best be illustrated with part of an interview we had with both of them together:

Rita: Ever since I was little I had to take care of my small cousins and other kids in the neighborhood. I used to like to take care of kids. It never bothered me when they cried or got into some kind of trouble. I used to do a lot of running errands to the store for my mother too, and I took care of a lot of things around the house. I always used to enjoy doing things like that.

Interviewer: Did you both take care of your little cousins?

Rita: We both did, but I did it more than Lucille.

Lucille: They always liked Rita better than me. I don't know why it was, but it was always Rita first and then me. I guess Rita just had a way with kids. She always liked to take care of kids. Rita took care of me too. (*She laughed.*) She fought my battles for me.

Interviewer: How was that?

Lucille: Well, just to give you an example, sometimes we'd be out swimming, and some kid would duck me for no good reason at all. Rita would come up and give them hell. She'd tell them they couldn't get away with something like that on her sister.

Rita: You see, I was always bigger than Lucille. I was a regular tomboy. It wasn't that I had to fight very often.

Most times I would just tell people, and they'd lay off Lucille.

Lucille: Yes, that's the way it was.

Rita (*sternly, to Lucille*): Don't bite your nails!

Lucille (*removes them quickly*): Well, I'm so nervous I have to do something.

It is hardly necessary to comment that in this case Lucille was the one who couldn't take it. In fact, she found the job so upsetting that she quit shortly after this interview, whereas Rita appeared always cheerful and in control of her situation.

To explore further this matter of initiative, let's compare Sue Tracy and Estelle Wolinski. Sue had been a waitress in this particular restaurant for over three years, which made her one of the longer service employees. She was an intelligent and very attractive girl. She had an unusually large number of steady customers. And yet, with all this in her favor, she was easily upset and broke down fairly often. Estelle had worked for only several months, not long enough to build up any following, and she was not attractive enough to make a favorable impression on customers through her appearance. Nevertheless, she took everything in her stride and never cried.

If we explore the patterns of human relations to which the two girls had become accustomed, we can explain their differing reactions.

There are two children in the Tracy family, Sue being four years younger than her sister. When Sue was growing up, her family moved around a great deal, so, she says, she did not make any close friendships with children. Most of her time was spent with adults, with whom she got along very well. Her father was a commercial artist. On her relations with her parents, she had this to say:

Well, when I was growing up, I was sick a lot of the time, and my mother was always there taking care of me. I got a lot of attention. I wasn't spoiled—that is, I don't think I was spoiled —but my parents tried to give me everything. That is, everything except a bicycle I wanted. Mother said she wouldn't give me that because I wasn't safe on the streets. Even now it's terrible the way I cross streets. I'm a regular jaywalker. It's just luck that I haven't been run over. I was knocked down by a car once, but I only got a bump out of it. Mother always would say that I wasn't safe on streets, and that's why I didn't get the bicycle. You see, they always treated me like the baby of the family.

In growing up, then, Sue had no experience in initiating action for others, was kept under close parental control, and became very dependent upon adult approval of her behavior. When customers failed to give her that approval, she was unable to manage the situation.

Estelle's background was quite different. She comes from a large family of Polish extraction, the seventh of nine children. When she was growing up, she always went around with a large gang of boys and girls. When she was with her group of girls, she took the lead. As she explained it,

Well, just to give you an example, suppose one of the girls said, "Let's go to a show." I might say, "Let's go boat riding," and then I'd try to convince the girls. I'd tell them, "Look, we put in a dollar between us, and we can go and get sodas, but if we go to a show, it'll be 35 cents apiece, and that'll be all we can do." I'd work on one girl to convince her first and then the two of us would work on somebody else. That way we'd get all the girls convinced. Most of the time they took my suggestions.

When we say that a girl has been a follower all her life, we mean that other people have been making her social adjustments for her. When she is placed in a position where that support is withdrawn, she breaks down. When we say that a girl has had a good deal of leadership experience, we mean that she has had to adjust herself and adjust others to a variety of social situations. She learns then to manipulate the restaurant situation so as to take some of the pressure off herself.

However, there are other factors besides leadership involved in this situation. Take the cases of Mary and Frances, small-town Ohio girls who came to the city for restaurant work. Mary had always been a follower and was very much dependent upon Frances. She explained herself in this way.

I always just stayed in the background. I followed along and did what other people wanted to do. I was always very shy when I was growing up. I still am a little shy, but I've changed a lot since being with Frances.

I admire Frances. She has so much initiative. I don't know what would have become of me if it hadn't been for Frances. I would still be stuck in that small town. I never would have had the nerve to go to the city by myself.

From the time that they left the small town, Mary and Frances had always lived and worked together. In the restaurant where we met them, they had begun work in the same dining room. This way they were able to work closely together, and Mary had no serious trouble. But then they were transferred into separate dining rooms and Mary began having trouble. One busy noon time, she had to leave the floor to cry. In the rest room she had hysterics. It was four days before she felt able to return to work. After that she and Frances were again set to work in the same dining room, and Mary had no further serious trouble.

There seem to be two interrelated factors involved here. Frances helped Mary with her work, and that lightened her load. However, it seems unlikely that the specific acts of helping out were the significant matter, for in the dining room where Mary broke down, the waitresses all prided themselves on the way they pitched in to help each other. Of

139

course, Mary and Frances knew each other so well that they were able to help each other more efficiently than any other person could, but it appears that a major part of this help was simply in the nature of social support—blowing off steam to a sympathetic audience, knowing that someone close to you understood your problems and was with you in spirit.

This suggests that social integration into the work group is of great importance in easing the nervous tensions of work. There is another sort of integration, the social adjustment outside the work situation, which is also important, as the case of Ann Lindstrom will indicate.

Ann was the leader of a large informal group of the younger waitresses, who always ate together in the afternoon and frequently got together outside of work. Growing up in Chicago in a Scandinavian neighborhood, she had been the leader of a group that had included only one other girl. She had never cried when with the gang. She could not have held her position if she had done so. Such a highly developed social initiative and such a strong conditioning against crying would seem to be a good guarantee against this sort of breakdown at work. Nevertheless, Ann did cry—and fairly often.

The problem in her case seemed to be two-sided involving downward social mobility and the disruption of her social ties outside the work situation. Her father had been a small businessman, ruined by the depression, who then became a factory worker. Ann had always been hostile to her mother, who tried to suppress the tomboy in her and make her a lady. In her late teens she married a young man who had been born in Europe, and this was thought to be a step down for her. Neighbors said to her mother, "Couldn't she do any better for herself than that?"

While Ann was very much on the defensive concerning her marriage, she nevertheless led a very active social life with her husband and his friends. Their home was the meeting place of the gang. However, after half a dozen years the marriage broke up. This cut her off not only from her husband but also from her gang.

Ann had been working in the credit department of a large firm, holding quite a responsible white-collar job. At about this time she had an accident that impaired her vision for close work, and she had to find a job that did not put such a strain on her eyes. It was that which led her into waitress work.

In the restaurant where we encountered her, she had become popular with a large group of employees, and yet she had not really accepted her new position. The first words she said to us were, "This is definitely not my type of work."

Finally, she suffered through a change in supervision. When she started work, she was close to her supervisor. She felt that the supervisor understood her, and the supervisor felt that she could count on Ann to help out whenever an extra bit of work needed to be done. Then there was a change, the new supervisor distrusted her, and thought that she was a bad influence for the other waitresses. Ann developed a great hostility toward the new supervisor, felt that she was under pressure from that source, and began to have more and more trouble in her work, until she told us, "It's getting to be just one crying jag after another." Shortly after this she quit.

The meaning of downward mobility to the waitress is again illustrated in the case of Alice Franklin. She was thirty-seven and unmarried, the fourth child in the family of a small-town schoolteacher. Her parents expected her to go to college, but at the time of her high-school graduation, they could not afford to send her away to the state university. Rather than start college in the local institution, she continued with a summer waitress job. In part, this was a rebellion against her parents, whom she considered puritanically strict.

Alice had been a waitress for 18 years. She had traveled all over the country, working in all types of restaurants. Since she had learned all the tricks of her trade, we might have expected her to handle her job without difficulty, and yet she was one of the few experienced girls who could not stand the strain without occasionally breaking down.

Alice had never been able to accept for herself the position of waitress. It seemed a serious comedown to one who had been brought up to think in terms of a professional career.

This had affected her social relations both on the job and outside of work. She had no intimate ties on the job. As she said,

I get along with them all right inside the restaurant, but I don't see many of them outside. You know, I don't believe in being too intimate with the people you work with. That leads to jealousy, and that leads to friction on the job. You begin going out with one particular girl, and then you have some kind of fight, and you take that right back to where you work. I think it's much better if you don't go around with the people you work with.

Even outside the work situation, she had few ties. She explained that the work tired her so much that when she was finished, she just wanted to rest. Thus, when she met the pressures of waitress work, she met them alone. Without any kind of social support, she could not stand up under the tension.

The importance of social mobility requires a further explanation. In a restaurant that prides itself on maintaining standards of refinement, the waitress learns the sort of behavior that is highly useful in moving up in the world. The restaurants where we gave particular attention to the crying waitress, recruit their girls largely from small towns, rural areas, and from the urban working class. To wait on tables properly, the girls must discard lower class or rural behavior and attitudes toward food, service, and etiquette, and adapt themselves to middle-class standards. More important still, they must learn to adjust themselves to their social superiors. They must appear to subordinate themselves and at the same time learn to manipulate people and situations to their own advantage. Girls who can absorb this sort of social learning find that their new pattern of behavior brings its own reward. Many former waitresses in this particular restaurant have married business or professional men or white-collar workers and have consolidated their social positions in the lower or even in the upper middle class.

The girl of middle-class background clearly faces a different situation. She finds herself taking orders from people whom she feels to be her equals and, in some cases, her inferiors. Nor do they recognize her former status. She finds it exceedingly difficult to adjust to this unaccustomed type of subordination.

This effort to explain the crying waitress has been long and involved—but necessarily so. We have long since ceased to look for *the cause* for any particular manifestation of human behavior. We always must deal with a number of interdependent variables, and we never see one of them operating quite isolated from the others. However, we have been able to discriminate three factors that seem of the greatest importance.

The waitress requires some leadership experience in order to take the play away from the customers and to fit them into the pattern of her work. She needs to be integrated into some group where she works and also in her life outside of work, so that she has some social support and some outlet for the tensions that arise in her job. (In some cases, the same group may serve to integrate her both at work and outside of it. We do not have enough data to know exactly what the social requirements are. We can only point to their importance.) And finally, the waitress needs security in her social position. If she is holding her own or moving up, she can adjust herself to the peculiar social pressures she faces much better than if she is downwardly mobile.

Of course, as we concentrate our attention upon the crying problem, we must remember that that is only one of a number of possible waitress reactions. To work out her problems, the waitress may (1) talk back to the customers, (2) yell at service pantry workers and bartenders, (3) break down and cry, get "the shakes," or other nervous reactions, (4) take the pressure off herself by controlling her customers, or (5) blow off steam to the supervisors.

It is clear that these first three reactions do not constitute solutions to the problem. We have, it is true, studied one lower class restaurant where a waitress informed us, "In this place the customer is always wrong, and he knows it—God bless him." In this restaurant we found no crying waitresses, but the middle-class restaurant cannot afford to allow its waitresses to tell the customers off.

When the waitress yells at people in other departments, she simply transfers the pressures to other people in the organization. When she cries, she has to leave the floor, and other waitresses must take over her station.

We have seen that a skillful waitress can take a good deal of pressure off herself through controlling her customers, but this in itself is not a solution to the problem; for there are always customers who cannot be controlled, and there are always waitresses who are not very successful in their attempts at control.

That raises a practical question for management: What can be done to improve the social skills of the waitress? Most managements have grappled with this problem in one form or another. Many of them have tried to solve it through inspirational talks on the psychology of salesmanship. There are several men who have made a nationwide reputation as salesmanship lecturers to employee groups, and many owners, managers, and supervisors have tried to serve this function in a more casual and less professional manner.

There are several difficulties inherent in this approach. In the first place, the principles of salesmanship are rather simple and generally familiar to most people. Therefore, even if employees get an emotional lift from a good talk on the subject, such talks become repetitious and boring if they are repeated often. Our experience so far is that salesmanship talks get a mixed response from employees. Some enjoy them. Others are unmoved. And some resent them. At best these programs are simply a temporary "shot in the arm."

The second difficulty is far more serious. We can illustrate it in this way. The salesmanship lecturer tells the waitresses that they will get along better with customers if they approach them with a pleasant smile. That is quite true. However, the assumption seems to be that the smile can be put on simply by an act of will. That is not true. A girl may be able to apply a smile to her face just as she puts on her lipstick, but unless she feels it inside her she won't be able to maintain it through the tensions of her work. Our research clearly shows that the girls who are successful with their smiles and pleasant manner really enjoy their work. While they may face many disagreeable situations, fundamentally they get pleasure out of pleasing and controlling customers. The other girls feel that customers are hostile and menacing forces, and an effective smile does not go with such a feeling.

The real problem then is: how can we help the girl to feel like smiling, to enjoy her work? A good deal of experimentation needs to be done in this area, but I think we can answer the question along general lines.

First it should be pointed out that this is not a problem peculiar to the restaurant industry. It crops up wherever the customer relationship is involved, and it is particularly important wherever the employee has the responsibility of making a sale, for in those cases management has a yardstick to measure the effectiveness of the salesman. When the records show that the salesman is not making his quota of sales, many managements take action in one of two ways. They may threaten the salesman with dire consequences if he does not improve. Or they may try to stimulate him through inspirational lectures.

Inspirational or not, a lecture is a lecture, and the salesman, who is falling down on the job because he is not adjusting well to customers or is preoccupied with some personal problem, will see in the lecture only just so much more pressure bearing down on him. Since he already feels worried and under pressure, more pushing from management only makes the situation worse.

This is not to argue that "pep talks" have no place in industry. The point is simply that pep talks don't solve human relations problems. When a man is under pressure, he cannot act with skill and confidence. Only when the pressure is relieved will he find inspiration in pep talks from management.

How then can management act to take the pressure off? That is a problem in supervision, and it has many aspects that we cannot take up here; but it should be emphasized that skillful supervision begins with giving employees an opportunity to talk their problems off their chests. If the worker cannot be allowed to express his emotions to the customer, then some other outlet must be provided, for bottled up emotions inevitably take their toll on the nervous system and reflect themselves in poor work performance.

The supervisor who looks upon nervous tensions as the inevitable products of human nature, as problems in the technical organization of work, or as problems in salesmanship will never be able to cope with the situation in a constructive manner. On the other hand, the supervisor who looks upon restaurant or factory as an organization of human relations, as a system of personal communication, will be able to make the necessary adjustments in order to minimize the frustrations and add to the satisfactions of work in industry.

Chapter VIII

ROLE OF UNION ORGANIZATION

MARK STARR

Educational Director,
International Ladies' Garment Workers' Union

THOSE of us who are hopeful that management and labor cooperation will continue beyond the war and play a vital part in solving postwar problems are not without some encouragement. Not so many years ago President Charles W. Eliot of Harvard glorified the strikebreaking "scab," who defied "trade union tyranny," as the apotheosis of the American ideals of courage and independence. Now Harvard University for the fourth year is running its Trade Union Fellowships to train trade union leaders after the La Follette Committee laid bare the near criminal agencies that supplied President Eliot's dubious hero.

A second encouraging sign of change is a new willingness to examine in detail the economic and social functions of the unions. From recent experiences it seems to me that someone should write a book on "The Movement Nobody Knows." Until 1944 there was no high-school text dealing specifically with the American labor movement. It was my privilege to cooperate with the distinguished social historian, Dr. Harold U. Faulkner, to write a text for the fourth year of high school. In the first and final chapters we set down the great contributions made by the labor unions to social welfare;

explained the economic protection and benefits provided by the unions; described their work in training skilled labor, in providing for the sick and aged, and in entertaining and educating their members. Many intelligent and widely read men and women have written in to say how completely uninformed they had been in regard to the constructive social phases of union activities.

My purpose here is to summarize briefly the role of union organization in relation to community welfare.

In the past employers have fought unions in the name of freedom. The law first treated the unions as trusts. For many years the unions were kicked around by the government and the courts until finally the Wagner Act was confirmed by the Supreme Court in 1937. For example, the big basic steel industry in the United States had been anti-union for 36 years. This meant that in the period of the New Deal, 1933-1943, the trade unions had much to make up. British union development in comparison had been slower and healthier. American industry was like a person suffering from a vitamin deficiency, and the National Labor Relations Board was forced feeding and vitamin pills to overcome our retarded growth in industrial relations. The process of making good for lost time has its drawbacks. With Sewell Avery not far distant from this University, there is some evidence, to use Prof. Selig Perlman's metaphor, that there will be attempts to annul the "shotgun marriage" forced upon capital and labor by President Roosevelt. But in the majority of cases the alliance has proved a happy one and the parties have improved by mutual acquaintance.

It went hard with some sections of business to see labor receiving any government aid. Others are even more alarmed when they see the union members using their votes to secure such things as the Fair Labor Standards Act and government guarantees against unemployment and of improved social security. But labor has studied the utilization of government by business interests for tariffs, subsidies, and tax relief. Labor, as an apt pupil, remembers the use of the power of government in 1933 to stem the depression when all else had failed, and remembers also the success of public enterprise and national unity in destroying Hitler. There may be temporary setbacks to the unions' advance. There may be a resurgence of the force and violence that have stained the pages of our social history, but labor banks upon the increasing social intelligence of the community to make necessary social changes by consent.

This is the over-all encouraging picture, but what of the individual worker? Why does he join a union? In the old days rebellion against exploitation was a major force. The smooth apologists for resistance to all change may dismiss the class struggle as nonexistent, but the boy born the other side of the tracks knows the difference between social groups. The layout of a mining town in Pennsylvania preaches class struggle more effectively than Karl Marx ever could. The general government statistics on the distribution of income and property ownership can be spelled out with little effort.

Out of the common exploitation and the common danger of the mine and mill came the feeling of brotherhood among the men and women who toil, which transcended any individual envy. Further, the unions express in modern fashion the protest against social injustice that is as old as history. For example, the Old Testament rings with eloquent denunciation of those who grind the faces of the poor. The speeches of the martyrs of the Haymarket affair, which occurred in Chicago in 1886, and of Eugene Debs are echoes lasting down to our own day and generation. "Our silence will be more powerful than the voices you strangle today," forecast August Spies. "Let the voice of the people be heard," Albert Parsons appealed, as he stood with Spies upon the Chicago scaffold. These rebels helped to arouse

150

the conscience of mankind although their protests seemed abortive. The sweatshop is disowned. Excesses of exploitation have been curbed. Safety and health regulations have advanced if slowly.

The unions are now more than an important movement of rebel workers. First, they satisfy a sense of belonging. Individuals lonely and afraid in a complex world they never made, to paraphrase A. E. Housman, find companionship and self-respect. The right of union membership is fundamental to the freedom of the worker. His union card is his passport to industrial rights. Even when unions cannot secure wage advances and better conditions, they prevent or reduce retreats. The official figures of the NLRB on elections show that workers once in a union do not choose to leave despite the abundant misinformation about unions to which they are subjected.

However, in these later New Deal days the unions are making organized attempts to explain to new members their rights and duties as union members, because increasingly men and women are not being tested by the old-time ordeal of the picket line to win the struggle for recognition. Nearly every union now distributes leaflets or pamphlets, runs classes for new members, or includes a new members' section in its journal to help the recruits cooperate intelligently in the procedures of collective bargaining. There are also many training classes and manuals for shop stewards and other union officers. Some of these manuals have been prepared, appropriately, with the assistance of the U. S. Department of Labor.

In addition to their basic function of safeguarding wages, hours, and work conditions, the unions in their early stages aided members in times of unemployment, sickness, and death. Their care for craftsmanship produced training classes and apprenticeship systems before public vocational and trade schools were developed. The wives of the members formed auxiliaries. Union parties, excursions, and meetings met the need for fellowship. Men and women "learned by doing" to speak in public and to write in their union journal. More ambitiously, unions ran their own study classes, their own ball teams, or formed and listened to their own union band and chorus. The record shows a wide variety of prewar cultural, recreational, and educational activities carried on by the unions, in addition to the work done by their journals and the practical learning arising from trade union experience. The International Ladies' Garment Workers' Union spends from $180,000 to $200,000 yearly on such educational work. Its groups range from ski clubs in Montreal to a hillbilly band in Texas; from compulsory classes for new members and those aspiring to be officers to institutes wherein its officers hear outstanding experts such as Henry J. Kaiser, Eric A. Johnston, Prof. Selig Perlman, and Elmo Roper.

More and more the modern union becomes concerned not only with wages and hours but with every phase of its members' lives. Particularly in the small towns of the United States, the union has become a community organization. The union hall and headquarters have become a center of social, cultural, and recreational activity. The union must provide information and guidance in matters of health, social security, family, housing, and political problems.

This, of course, is not to minimize the importance of economic security. It is useless talking about a fuller and better life unless that life has an adequate economic basis in decent wages, a working week that permits some leisure, and an organization in which the worker can secure some say in the conditions under which he obtains his livelihood. Trade unions, assisting men and women to obtain decent living standards, prevent the creation of problems that otherwise would fall upon the social agencies. Insofar as the union tries to improve the standards of life, it is making an im-

152

portant contribution to social welfare and to the happiness of the community. All progressive citizens can help chambers of commerce and communities to avoid the shortsighted acceptance of runaway shops from other areas, because these industrial gypsies are trying to avoid decent labor standards built up in organized areas. Trade union leaders as well as representative employers should sit on all public planning boards. And incidentally some of the local committees for economic development have already secured union participation.

While unions have always emphasized economic gains, their broad social welfare interest has firm roots in the early history of the trade union movement. Leo Perlis, National Director of the CIO War Relief Committee, has shown that health and welfare planning for the community is not a departure from the original trade union philosophy.

It is simply another step forward in the evolution of the organized labor movement. As long ago as 1827, the Mechanics' Union of Trade Associations, meeting in Philadelphia, declared that its "real object" among other things, "is to promote, equally, the happiness, prosperity and welfare of the whole community . . . and to assist . . . in establishing a just balance of power, both mental, moral, political and scientific, between all the various classes and individuals which constitute society at large."

It is obvious that more than 100 years ago workers conceived of the trade union as an instrumentality for the "happiness, prosperity, and welfare of the whole community" far beyond the immediate confines of wages, hours, and working conditions. The conception of a pure and simple trade unionism circumscribed, functionally, by the eternal class struggle for the highest possible wages, lowest possible hours, and best possible working conditions is a figment of the imagination and has no basis in fact. Unions, from the very beginning, have expressed, in one form or another, the concern of working men and women with problems outside the factory gates. Labor

153

took to politics, for example, as far back as 1829 when the New York Working Men's Party was organized, and in 1830, the Working Men's Advocate declared: "Your fathers of the Revolution secured to you a form of government which guarantees to you, almost universally, the elective franchise. . . . If you possess the rights of freemen, you have exercised them as the privileges of slaves. . . . Awake, then, from your slumbers."

While trade unionists have always been concerned with community problems, the tremendous growth of the labor movement in recent years has given union leaders positions of power and influence in America society and has emphasized their responsibility for thinking and acting in terms of a broad social program. In such efforts, unions need the help of social agencies and of all citizens who are concerned with community problems. The more progressive and active the union, the greater its opportunity for mutually beneficial cooperation with social agencies. Union members, be it noted, are also citizens and taxpayers; they want public money spent wisely according to farsighted plans. Society cannot afford shortsighted economies that would scrap important social services, and the trade unions can help influence public opinion upon this matter.

Many years ago the British Charity Organization Society was described in these satirical words:

> Organized charity measured and iced
> In the name of a cautious statistical Christ.

While some workers still are reluctant to have any dealings with social workers, much of the old distrust has been eliminated in the development of modern social work. The social worker is no longer a detective who tracks down poverty as a crime.

Once the mentally sick were beaten and put in straitjackets, but now we use other methods in treating the insane. Likewise the victims of poverty were once coerced and maltreated or grudgingly given handouts. Once poor people were imprisoned for debt. Now we know better and the trade unions, by helping to prevent poverty, can cooperate with modern, intelligent social agencies. Unions can do much to prevent social evils that social workers are often vainly trying to "mop up."

The social worker and the social agency, instead of being an ambulance corps for a disordered society, can become architects of social planning. They can prevent the problems of delinquency and other grave social evils by attacking them at their roots.

Social work went ahead in the United States compared to other countries because of the problems created by the immigrant in the large cities. This original urgency has lessened considerably; but there remains the problem of orienting the children of the immigrants, and indeed our native sons and daughters, into these ways of industrial democracy in which capital and labor unions meet as equals to discuss, not private charity or individual benevolence, but their rights and duties in relation to industry. We still suffer from racketeering "hangovers" created by the get-rich-quick psychology, but newer ideals of honesty and community welfare are being established.

Social workers can cooperate with the unions and vocational schools in the difficult and complex problem of inducting young workers into industry. The social worker in the past was too often engrossed in the study of the individual and his problems, without relating individual problems to social problems. Very often the trade union leader is blamed for refusing to drop the bars to the entrance of new candidates into industry because the social worker does not understand the reason for those restrictions and defenses, built up as the result of many years of difficult struggle. The intelligent union leader and the social worker can get together for vocational training based on the real needs and prospects of industry and not on the optimistic hopes of employers who wish to overcome justifiable restrictions set down by the union and to swamp the industry with cheap juvenile labor.

This may bring to mind examples of allegedly antisocial restrictions by unions—the Petrillo royalty on records, the painters' opposition to the spray gun, the miners' opposition to hydroelectric plants, the building trades workers' objections to prefabricated houses, etc. It should never be forgotten that the majority of unions do not oppose technical improvements and new processes. However, the union regulations result from long and bitter experience of industrial dangers and the fear of unemployment. None of us welcomes our personal obsolescence. The iceman, argue the musicians, is not compelled to make the refrigerator. We do not give up our job to the other fellow unless we have or hope to have a better one. Workers have invested their lives in the accumulation of specific skills. If dismissal wages, retraining and placement plans, improved social security and alternative employment opportunities were provided, the community would be more justified in criticising the so-called "feather-bedding" and other union restrictions. A sign of the new times is the "efficiency clause" in the current agreement of the New York dressmakers that gives the worker the right to complain to the impartial chairman of the industry if the employer does not maintain efficient methods. Noteworthy too is the work of the ILGWU Industrial Engineering Department, which advises the union members and the employers on new work methods and machines. Other unions now use industrial engineers to evaluate new processes.

The success of cooperation between management and labor in the industrial war effort has already made history. General Eisenhower summed it up:

The production of our people has won high praise. . . . There is not a battlefield of Europe where it has not been of decisive importance. You sent us the most—and the best.

It will be tragic if this cooperation is not continued and expanded into peacetime through the charter proposed jointly by Eric Johnston, Phil Murray, and William Green. The war has accentuated productivity and concentration of industry. Payment of debts, financing of industrial expansion, and shifts in industry through foreign trade are only a few of the problems now to be faced.

One encouraging factor making for better public relations is the integration of the unions into community life through their gifts and active cooperation with the Red Cross, USO, War Relief funds, Community Chests, War Bond drives and similar activities. For example, CIO members in Detroit gave $1,150,000 to the 1944 community war fund drive. In Pittsburgh the CIO contribution was $736,507 and the nationwide CIO contribution to the 1944 campaign was about $20,000,000. The three-year CIO total to war and home-front relief and welfare is estimated to be over 85 million dollars.

With their legal status secure, unions were able to play an important role not only in the plants but outside. This was not entirely new, for the unions had already a record in the attainment of public education, of opening up free lands, and in regulating women and child labor. What had been good for labor in higher wages and shorter hours had been good for the community. But in wartime, problems of health, housing, cost of living, medical care, and civilian defense demanded united effort. The unions' record has not yet been fully appreciated.

Matthew Woll, President of the Labor League for Human Rights, official relief arm of the American Federation of Labor, summed up the AFL record in these words:

AFL members have contributed more than 120 million to War Community Chests and the Red Cross since 1942.

AFL volunteers serving on local War Community Chests and Red Cross Committees increased from 2,406 to 3,856 in the past year.

The AFL is now represented on 835 War Community Chests and Red Cross chapter committees this year, compared with 681 last year.

Speaking before the 1944 National Conference of Social Work, Mr. Woll said,

As far as labor is concerned, we can say today that the first steps in a constructive program of cooperative action have already been taken. The working people of the United States as a whole are now assuming their fair share of the financial responsibilities of social work, and what is still more important, they are beginning to assume a growing responsibility for its planning and administration. We have in various parts of the United States today a new phenomenon, the labor participation committee, designed to bring labor and the social worker together in an organized fashion for the sake of their mutual cooperation in solving problems of community welfare.

These committees will attempt to develop labor participation in social planning and the organization and administration of health, welfare, and other community services where labor is adequately represented. They will study methods and possibilities of extending such services so that the needs of the entire community—labor and nonlabor—may be better served. These committees will work toward combining the efforts and resources of welfare agencies and organized labor in building sound, functioning, truly representative community programs.

A further function of these labor participation committees will be to develop mutual understanding of the problems of social workers and the problems of organized labor, where these two mesh. They will attempt to disseminate among members of trade unions a greater knowledge of the services provided by social agencies. Then, too, they will interpret the aims and views of labor to social agencies and advise them as to the best method of proceeding with union members.

But, most important of all, it will be the function of these labor participation groups to see that the needs of the working population in every community, as workers, are recognized in total community planning. We are seeking the establishment of labor participation committees and representation of labor in the councils of social agencies, and I predict that through these means a much broader base for welfare activity will be developed in the very near future.

The National CIO War Relief Committee, formed in 1941, reported in its excellent pictorial,[1] "The Story of Citizen CIO," its own diverse record of activity in 1944. Through its 24 area offices, it raised funds to fight Fascism on a minimum basis of 12 hours' pay per year. The grand total raised in 1943-1944 was $261,307,825 of which more than half went to local community chests. Reflecting labor's influence as a big giver, CIO representatives on social agency boards went up from 90 to about 4,000 serving on local, state, and Federal organizations.

The AFL and CIO cooperated in sponsoring special projects, such as rest break homes and hospitals in China, Soviet Russia, and Britain. They helped the refugees and the underground movement. The Labor League for Human Rights and the National CIO War Relief were recognized by the National War Fund as important agencies and were each allocated $350,000 to maintain their regional and central staffs.

The war accentuated the old needs for child care centers, housing, medical care, transport facilities, education, recrea-

[1] In November, 1945, Philip Murray, CIO president, announced that the CIO War Relief Committee had become the National Community Services and that the new emphasis of the committee's work would be cooperation with public and private welfare agencies on the community level.

tion, accident prevention in workshop and home, and vocational training. The unions assisted, sometimes through labor-management committees, sometimes independently.

Trade unions arranged X-ray chest examinations, ran children's camps, sent soldiers parcels, letters, leaflets, and manuals, and helped and advised both inductees and returned veterans. Contributions to blood banks and purchases of bonds were effectively organized by the unions. The general totals are hard to obtain because individual unions make grants directly to war relief funds and projects. For example, *News of China* for June, 1945, reprints the architect's drawing for an orphanage to which the ILGWU gave $100,000 in 1944.

The most outstanding of many labor canteens is the Philadelphia USO-Labor Plaza, which has played host since its start in 1943 to 1,500,000 service men and women. Here the AFL and the CIO joined to provide the construction labor, maintenance funds, and hostess personnel. On the West Coast the AFL unions have run for more than three years the Holywood Canteen, directed by Bette Davis, outstanding actress and union member. These are only typical of what individual unions have done in this community for the armed forces.

Currently the shift of interest is to problems of veterans and of the unemployed created by cutbacks in wartime production. Some large locals of the United Auto Workers have appointed an employment director. The unions recognize the dangers in the attempts to divide the veterans and trade unionists despite the fact that over three million union members served in the armed forces. Special work also is being done to combat discrimination against minorities.

All this activity gave the labor unions a new and much improved community status. The YMCA lagged badly for many years behind the YWCA industrial department in sympathy and support for labor unions, but now it is getting from and giving assistance to organized labor. The Lansing, Mich., YMCA has CIO and AFL representatives on its board of directors, and this sort of community participation by unions may be expected to develop still further in the future.

The new relations with social work agencies originated the union counselor to deal with *out-plant* difficulties as the shop chairman or steward dealt with *in-plant* problems. Union counseling grew up in the UAW in 1943-1944 partly because in some plants the personnel counselors were antiunion. Some of them were even placed in the women's rest room to prevent loitering. At best there is the danger of the revival of paternalism. If the boss knows about a worker's home and his personal troubles, he may ditch him.

To meet these out-plant problems, some advocated the organization of social services by the unions themselves. It was felt that certain social agencies had pursued antiunion policies under the domination of employers on their boards of directors. However, setting up competing social agencies would be a costly enterprise, and the growing representation of CIO and AFL unions on the boards of these agencies seemed to offer new possibilities for a program of cooperation free from employer bias.

Both the CIO and the AFL have sponsored union counseling programs that have been developing rapidly all over the country. Union members have been trained in special classes to handle problems of housing, health, unemployment compensation, and many other matters.

At first it was thought that the sole function of the union counselor should be to refer the client to the agency that was equipped to handle the problem in question. However, experience has shown that the counselor who merely refers them to an agency is rarely consulted by his fellow workers. The members do not readily go by themselves to social agencies, and they seem to expect the counselor to represent them in this relationship as the union steward does in their in-plant problems. Furthermore, the mere giving of advice leaves many problems unsolved, for the worker often has a greater need to get his problem off his chest, talking it out to a sympathetic and skillful listener.

It has also been found that counseling, on a purely individualistic basis, has serious limitations, for many of the problems faced by workers are total community problems. A housing shortage, inadequate medical care, and other matters of broad concern cannot be solved through individual counseling, but when the counselors bring these problems up for discussion in union meetings, they provide the union with the information and drive necessary for bringing organized labor's influence to bear upon the social welfare program of the community.

We live in a society so complex that no one of us is able to solve his own problems completely unaided. We need guideposts through the complicated structures of government, industry, and the community, and we need to rely upon others for friendly aid along the way. The union counseling program is designed to meet that need. A new program still in its experimental stage, it nevertheless offers great possibilities for the adjustment of the problems faced by workers in their lives outside of working hours.

In some areas the unions have made experiments in employing professional social workers. The best of such plans is run by the National Maritime Workers Union, CIO, in New York, in cooperation with the United Seamen's Service and the War Shipping Administration. Four social workers staff this personnel service department and advise 60 to 80 workers daily. In other instances, family welfare agencies have placed staff members in union halls just as housing, social security, accident compensation, unemployment compensation, and income tax experts have been utilized to meet special needs. The Social Service Employees Union

(UOPWA-CIO) has naturally promoted joint activity although its political coloration in some cases is not conducive to cooperation from the AFL.

Since February, 1945, the AFL Service Bureau of the New York War Chest has helped union members to solve their personal problems. Typical difficulties include financial crises at home, care of dependent children, vocational guidance, recreation, prevention of delinquency, and nursing care in illnesses like tuberculosis, heart disease, and cancer. The bureau acts as a link between local AFL unions and the social agency most appropriate in a given situation, and maintains a working relationship with over a thousand public or privately operated agencies. Through it, unions are enabled to be of maximum aid to their members in outside problems as well as in employment protection.

So far 15 cities have set up such information centers, which serve the AFL trade and craft unions working often in scattered small industries.

The mutual benefits to social work and to trade unions of this new integration of union activity into community life can be easily imagined. Social workers number only 70,000 compared to 133,000 clergymen and over a million teachers. The trade unions have the resources to influence the community to take action to the improvement of social welfare.

Unions have already branched out into other activities to supplement their original functions of workshop protection. They have developed credit unions to rescue their members from the loan shark. They have set up committees and conferences to overcome racial and religious discrimination. There is a small but fast increasing interest in consumer cooperatives to help control the cost of living by eliminating the middleman and to apply collective bargaining on the model of the Rochdale pioneers. Some unions, such as the Amalgamated Clothing Workers, the Hosiery Workers, the

Shipbuilding Workers, and the UAW, have done notable work in promoting model housing schemes.

In recent years unions have increasingly begun the provision of medical care of their members. Some unions have been long active in this field. The Union Health Center of the ILGWU was started back in 1913 and its most recent report shows that, while 1,234 visits were made for medical advice in 1913, the total had increased to 116,185, 30 years later. The Union Health Center occupies more than 20,000 square feet of a modern building in the garment center of New York, easily accessible to workers, who come during the lunch hour or when the working day is over. In 1943, 85 men and 22 women physicians served the center—4 on full-time basis and 67 on a permanent part-time basis. The ACW in Chicago has also maintained a similar center. The UAW and other newer unions have set up a medical institute. Union journals currently abound with details of new plans. These health plans are only in their infancy. Many unions, which could not get an increase in wages because of the Little Steel formula, secured health and retirement funds. Vacations with pay lead to union holiday homes.

It is a logical development that workers are now alerting themselves on the question of accident prevention. What good are high wages if the worker is liable to drop dead from high blood pressure? What good are shorter hours if the worker is too incapacitated by illness or accident to enjoy them?

If the union tries to be a way of life for its members, it must fight all that makes for premature death. Thus the unions at the present time are logically widening their activities into the field of public and private health. The ILGWU now has health and vacation plans covering over 200,000 workers. The union has now established the Welfare and Health Benefits Department. Plans are being made to run regional conferences to show the workers that

care of health and accident prevention pay good dividends—
that life can be bought—and generally to awaken them to
cherish their health.

Along with such expanded community activity, unions
naturally are taking an increasingly active interest in politics and in governmental policy. There can be little doubt
that there will be more social planning and not less, as the
years pass by. A nation can ill afford again to lose 200
billion dollars by the unemployment of men and machines
as it did during the years 1930-1937, according to the
National Resources Committee. How badly we need social
control and social planning for freedom, adopted by intelligent men and women of their own free will, is evidenced also
by the gross inequalities in education and health facilities
and the continuing maldistribution of wealth, which puts
many families beneath the income level necessary for standards of health and decency. The report made by Senator
Claude Pepper on July 15, 1945, showed that wartime prosperity has not ended low wages. The report, in urging a
65-cent hourly minimum, said:

Substandard rates of pay have meant poverty, ill-health, and
degradation for millions of American citizens. Witnesses before the subcommittee graphically described the privation and
suffering to which they have been condemned by earnings of
40 cents and 50 cents an hour.

Malnutrition, sickness, insufficient medical care, poor housing, inadequate clothing, bare homes, limited education, meager
cultural and recreational advantages, continuous struggle and
lack of opportunity are characteristic of the lives of these
Americans who are not receiving a living wage for their toil.

Unions have long realized that social problems, such as
delinquency and crime, must be met in terms of an enlight-
ened social policy. In New York City we have the bad habit
of letting our district attorneys use their recurring prose-

cutions of gangsters as a ladder to nationwide fame and political ambition. So dazzling are their claims to omniscience that the eyes of the public are diverted from seeing that slums, bad education, unemployment, and lack of civic conscience continue to produce gangsters as before in readiness for the next potential political meteor.

The political machines of Chicago, Kansas City, New York City, Jersey City, and elsewhere have always done enough "illegitimate social work" to retain votes but at too great cost in corruption and graft. Unions are undertaking to bring their influence to bear in the political arena to see that politicians are made to face the social and economic ills of our society and to formulate constructive policies to eliminate the causes of maladjustment.

As the trade unions enter into new fields of social and political activity, the tasks of leadership become increasingly complicated. To meet these new responsibilities, unions are beginning to build up training programs for their officers, and some are even setting down educational qualifications for would-be officers. The universities are currently stepping in to help the unions train their members. Among others, the University of Illinois, the University of Michigan, Harvard University, Cornell University, the University of Chicago, and Pennsylvania State College, are establishing industrial relations schools or centers.

A pattern of wide variety is thus in the making: participation in community efforts for the USO and the Red Cross and Community Chests both in getting and spending contributions; use of professional social workers in personal advice bureaus, supplemented by training of union shop counselors informed about the welfare agency resources of their own neighborhood; independently financed efforts by unions to provide medical care and schemes maintained jointly with the employers or paid for by the latter through pay-roll percentage deductions; last but not least, agitation for wider

166

Federal and state schemes of social security on the lines of the Wagner-Murray-Dingell Bill to supplement what the unions are doing directly in this field.

Many of the items cited here to illustrate the expanding role of trade unions are small in themselves. Yet pieced together they make a new pattern of helpful group activity and collective self-help too often previously ignored but now continued and extended in the hour of national crisis. They indicate a broadened concept of a trade union's functions. In their long-time result, they indicate the possibility of conscious adaptation to wider community needs for social well-being. According to Adolph Sturmthal, "The tragedy of European labor" was the "stalemate of conflicting social forces" in which organized labor could not elevate itself from a pressure group to a national community force, uniting all men of clear social vision and good will. We should not let that happen here.

If the real activities of union organization are understood by the farmers, the members of the professions, and the white-collar workers, then the future role of labor unions with their great numerical strength may be even more important, as we consciously guide and direct our social evolution combining creative planning with the Bill of Rights.

Chapter IX

THE BASIS OF INDUSTRIAL CONFLICT

Frederick H. Harbison

NOW that war is over we are faced with strikes and industrial turmoil. Some companies are anxious to regain control from the unions over so-called "management prerogatives" and are ready to "slug it out" with labor. Unions see a bitter struggle for survival, and many labor officials are authorizing strikes to force concessions from management. At the moment, the prospects for harmonious labor-management relations throughout the land are not very promising.

Faced with a situation of this kind, our first impulse is to pass a law to regulate union-employer relationships—to set up governmental machinery for arbitration and compulsory investigation of labor disputes—to outlaw strikes in vital industries—to define by legislation the *rights* of employees, the *rights* of unions, and the *rights* of management. In short, there is a tendency to try to ensure *responsibility* in industrial relations by making *irresponsibility* illegal.

Any thoughtful student of industrial relations, however, is aware of the fallacies of such an "ostrich policy," yet our congressmen continually advertise such measures as "cure-alls" for industrial strife, and many of us are willing to accept these quack remedies to relieve ourselves temporarily of the distasteful task of grappling with more fundamental issues.

168

What are the focal points of conflict between employers and organized labor—wage rates, annual wage plans, seniority, the union shop, "accumulated" grievances, or other issues? Certainly, all these issues are the *stated* reasons for many strikes; they are the obvious reasons, but there are more basic focal points of disagreement. We must go much deeper to diagnose the underlying motivations.

Our analysis is based on two assumptions: (1) that the power and prestige of organized labor will not diminish appreciably in the postwar period, which may be open to some question; and (2) that the postwar economy will be geared primarily to private enterprise, about which there is very little doubt.

As to the first assumption, the power and prestige of organized labor are at an all-time high. Nearly 15 million workers are currently members of AFL, CIO, or independent unions, about three times the previous membership peak at the end of the First World War. Unionization is not confined to a few crafts and industries as it was after the last war; it has spread to all types of wage earners, semiskilled and unskilled, throughout all types of industry and commerce, and is reaching out into new fields almost every day. Those who predict a sharp decline in union membership following the war similar to that which followed the First World War make an obvious mistake in drawing parallels between 1918 and 1945. In the last war, unionization and collective bargaining were encouraged by the government only as temporary wartime measures, whereas a permanent national policy favorable to unions was adopted many years prior to the Second World War. The unions of today were strongly entrenched long before Pearl Harbor. They have leadership, financial resources, and political prestige today that eclipse any strength they possessed in 1918.

Furthermore, there is clear-cut evidence that most American workers are strongly behind unions *in principle*, even though they seem to be reluctant to give them voluntary support in the absence of an "issue" that affects their vital job interests.

Our second assumption is that the system of private enterprise will survive. The left-wing groups in this country have never developed the leadership or prestige of their counterparts in other parts of the world. American workers are interested primarily in individual *rights* or equities in jobs, and, although they are conscious of their status as wage earners, they are not as a group militantly class-conscious in the sense of being opposed to capitalism. To the extent that private enterprise can provide jobs at reasonable rates of pay, workers and unions in this country, by and large, seem prepared to string along with the employers. If employers as a group should launch a concerted drive to lower wages and oust unions, it is possible, of course, that they might thereby help to create a more class-conscious, revolutionary labor opposition. If our present system, furthermore, cannot provide sufficient jobs in the future, it might conceivably be supplanted by another system offering more promise of so doing.

If unions are here to stay and if our economy continues to center around private enterprise, it is obvious that collective bargaining must be made to operate effectively within the framework of a free society.

One basic reason for industrial strife in this country is the struggle between management and organized labor for prestige with workers, which often degenerates into a sort of "cutthroat competition" for employee loyalty. Most employers want their employees to feel that they need not join a union to get a square deal from management or to protect their job interests. Some executives, in fact, regard a favorable vote for a union in a labor board election as an act of "desertion" on the part of those who were formerly "loyal" employees. Frequently, we hear management complaining

170

that a union drives a wedge between the company and its employees. Many employers look upon unions and their leaders as *competing for* rather than *representing* the interests of workers. In dealing with a union, management is constantly aware of the "silent third party"—the workers whose interests, the company feels, are not necessarily represented by the union. Management seldom likes the union to take credit for any concessions that the company is willing to make to employees.

Labor leaders, on the other hand, hold that jobs can be safeguarded and opportunities for employment enhanced only through union action, and that a union is the only organization that can be concerned with the interests of workers. Union officers usually point out that management cares very little about the well-being of its employees and that the company is interested only in getting out the work irrespective of the consequences to the workers. Furthermore, union leaders bitterly condemn unilateral action taken by management to improve the condition of workers as an "antilabor" drive to "kill off the union with kindness." Accordingly, unions often seek to undermine workers' confidence in the motives of management by campaign tactics designed to spread hatred and disrespect for the authority of the company.

The antagonism and name calling that are so prevalent in American labor-management relations stem in large measure from labor-management competition for allegiance of workers. Our interviews with American workers, supported by almost all the opinion polls, indicate quite clearly that a worker's life, hopes, and expectations center around his job. To the extent that a union can secure a wage raise or increase the security of his job, he will give it his active support. The vast majority of union members are interested in immediate tangible benefits. In return for their union dues, they want value received. To the extent that management is able to deliver the "pork chops" without union pressure, the worker is often ready to shift his allegiance to the company. In short, a large proportion of American workers are willing to let management and organized labor compete for their support. They are at the same time suspicious of management and sometimes distrustful of the union leadership, particularly when a question of compulsory membership or payment of dues arises. During the last 10 years the trend of allegiance of workers appears to be toward unions rather than management, although there are many noteworthy exceptions to this general trend.

Viewed in this context, some of the issues in labor-management relations, such as "maintenance of membership" and the "union shop" can be focused more clearly. Employers oppose making union membership a condition of employment primarily to prevent the growth of strong labor organizations. The employer, of course, opposes the union shop because it may result in the union securing an economic stranglehold on the company by control of the labor supply. He also hates to see his workers taken over completely into the union camp. Union leaders press for the union shop because of a recognition that they cannot persuade all workers, in the face of company competition, to become union members. Accordingly, they seek to compel allegiance to the union by making employment dependent on support of the union.

Another focal point of conflict is the question of discipline—a factor that underlies the widespread unrest in the large automobile plants of Detroit. Management naturally wants to retain its right to discharge workers who do not meet prescribed standards and to promote those best qualified for advancement. In order to maintain efficiency and to retain their *status* as managers, executives want workers to look to the company, and not to the union, for criticism or approval. Although the union, too, may have an interest in efficient operations, it usually wants to share these so-called "management prerogatives" so that workers will be less dependent on decisions of the company. Union demands for seniority rules, for example, are primarily motivated by a desire to limit management's discretion over layoffs and promotion and to shift the control of jobs, which are so vital to workers, away from the company to the union. As competition between unions and companies for the support of workers becomes more acute, unions exert more and more pressure to limit management's freedom in exercising its prerogatives. Thus we can see the motivating force behind demands for the determination of promotions by seniority rather than by management discretion, for changes in the wage rates only by mutual consent, for joint labor-management committees, and for protective working rules of all kinds.

Now these motivations are so deeply imbedded in the thinking of company executives and labor leaders that it is useless to try to resolve the issue by defining the *rights* of management and the *rights* of unions. In fact, the very talk of *rights* often accentuates conflict by inducing each side to take an uncompromising stand on "principles." Human relations problems will never be solved through legal enactment.

Some observers contend that this basic conflict cannot be resolved—that either management must win the struggle by weakening or eliminating unions or organized labor must win a decisive victory over management and take over the very reins of industry. There are groups on both sides who want a showdown on this issue. Thus, there is, unfortunately, a basis for continuing industrial conflict.

Most employers and union leaders, however, do not hold such a gloomy concept of labor relations. They hope that collective bargaining can be made to work under certain conditions. What are these conditions and can they be fulfilled?

In examining cases where cooperative and productive relationships exist between management and organized labor, we usually find that the employer has accepted *labor organizations as a constructive force* and as an integral part of industrial organization. For its part, the union has accepted the function of management in directing private enterprise and has recognized that jobs are dependent upon the continuation of profitable operation of the business. The attitude on each side is one of wholehearted acceptance of the function of the other. In such cases, there is little "jockeying for position" for influence with workers, and the workers usually have confidence in both the company and the union.

A company that accepts unions wholeheartedly looks upon them as providing better means of communication between workers and company officials and as an incentive to better management. One company president recently expressed this idea to me in this way: "The unions certainly irritate us and the leadership at one of our plants is pretty terrible. On the other hand, we in management recognize that we are doing a better job today because of the existence of unions in our plants, for the simple reason that unions bring to light deficiencies in management that would otherwise be overlooked and hence left uncorrected." Implicit in this attitude is a recognition of the function of unions in providing better communication with workers.

Also implicit in such acceptance of unions is an understanding that the company is not trying to find a way of making unions unnecessary. The company recognizes that the setting of wage rates, the establishment of criteria for layoffs and advancement, the setting of production standards, and other matters falling within the scope of so-called "management prerogatives" affect workers as human beings, and, as human beings, workers want to be consulted about

174

these matters and seek some voice in their determination. Companies that have accepted unions are usually convinced that the *participation of workers through their unions* in the determination of policies that affect them tends to increase efficiency and to strengthen rather than weaken management. Avoiding taking unilateral action in such matters, the management banks on its leadership "ability" rather than its prerogatives to initiate action. It frankly acknowledges the role of the union in bringing about improvements in working conditions.

You almost never find companies accepting unions in this manner, however, unless the unions involved have a constructive attitude toward management. In a situation where a union has wholeheartedly accepted management, you seldom find experienced and intelligent organizers appealing to workers through a campaign of mudslinging and jeering. Where an employer is willing to "play ball" with the unions, slander campaigns are usually ineffective, and often sow the seeds of future discord within the union, for workers trained and coached to disrespect authority soon show the same feeling toward their own union leaders.

In addition to an attitude of respect for the company, you will also find that the union leadership involved usually has made up its mind that private enterprise is here to stay, and that in the interest of the workers and the union membership, there must be cooperation with management to increase the size of the total earnings "pie" in addition to reaching agreement on the proportionate slice that goes to labor. While participating in the setting of wage rates, the making of time and motion studies, the determination of production standards and layoff and promotion policies, there is a recognition that these are essential functions that must be performed efficiently if the company is to maintain its competitive status and hence be in position to maintain or expand employment. In such cases, the unions are usually described as "cost conscious" in that they recognize that the employer must constantly improve plant efficiency and make a reasonable profit in order to stay in business and thus to provide jobs for the membership. Concrete examples of this type of attitude by labor are found, for example, in the clothing industry, where the unions have actively cooperated with employers to lower unit costs to allow expanded production at lower prices.

The initial observations set forth above are the result of a rather careful interview analysis of 50 situations where "good" relationships existed between the union and the company. It was quite apparent in all these cases, in contrast to those where there was a great deal of friction in the relationship, that the top management and top union leadership had accepted wholeheartedly each other's status and function in a free society. In some cases, the employer had signed a union shop contract, but in others there were no stipulations requiring that employment be dependent on union membership. In all these cases, the union shop was not an important issue—nor was there fundamental difference on questions such as discharge and seniority. *This leads one to conclude that when the status and function of each side are clearly recognized by the other, some of these bitterly contested issues in union-management relations may cease to be focal points of controversy.*

We should not jump to the conclusion, however, that an attitude of wholehearted acceptance of unions by company executives automatically induces an attitude of constructive collaboration on the part of union officers. A company executive can change his mind about fighting unions, and his status position in management need not be disturbed. A union leader who collaborates with a cooperative employer, on the other hand, is frequently charged by a segment of the membership with "selling out to the boss." Moreover, a

176

union dominated by extremists is likely to take advantage of a company policy of management-union cooperation.

Likewise a "cost-conscious" labor leader is often afraid to initiate a policy of union-management cooperation unless he is sure that management is willing to work hand and glove with the union on all matters connected with the jobs of the workers in the plant. In short, each side wants the other to "reform" first. Practically speaking, however, employers are usually in a better position to initiate a policy of co-operation because their status and position are not so dependent on pleasing a constituency as that of union leaders, who must weigh the political repercussions of every action.

Actually, a good many top employers and top labor leaders are already in substantial agreement on the fundamentals of good labor-management relations. The trouble is that the attitude is not always accepted down the line by supervisors and foremen and by local union officers and members.

A constructive attitude by a top company officer does not become a constructive management policy until after it is thoroughly understood and communicated throughout the entire management hierarchy of superintendents and foremen. This is often a long, tedious process, for adjustments in status, outlook, and thinking are required by hundreds, sometimes thousands, of individuals. Foremen, long taught to think of labor leaders as racketeers and labor exploiters, can't suddenly be expected to "fraternize" with union stewards who may be responsible for a certain deterioration in their status. Within the union, furthermore, the shift from militancy to collaboration may necessitate not merely a change in attitude on the part of the union leadership but perhaps a complete change of union officers. Unions theoretically are governed from the bottom up while corporations are governed supposedly from the top down.

Therefore, effective union-management relations, granted the existence of constructive motivation at the top, are dependent upon acceptance and understanding of the relationship by the *management and union rank and file.* Here we have a problem in education—in communication—in human relations. The training techniques required to resolve this problem are beyond the scope of this book. In passing, however, we should note that because of the "upward line of authority" within labor organizations, the education of the union rank and file is a more difficult and complex undertaking than the training of management's rank and file. To be sure, there may be cliques in many companies that hamper the development of a consistent and unified labor policy. But these are not so pronounced as the "political parties" within unions with conflicting "platforms" for action.

The growth of cooperative labor-management relations, accordingly, will be a slow process and there are likely to be many setbacks. We can expect, as experience has demonstrated, that good relationships will develop more rapidly in smaller plants than in the larger organizations because adjustments in status and changes of attitude are required by a relatively smaller number of persons who may have more intimate day-to-day contact with each other.

Utopia in labor-management relations, however, *cannot* be achieved alone by employer acceptance of unions and union recognition of management, *even if there is adequate understanding and acceptance of such a policy up and down the line.* There are other prerequisites for constructive labor-management cooperation that lie outside the scope of direct labor-management relationships in the plant.

In the first place, collaboration between labor and management is not always desirable. Cooperative relationships between companies and unions can be perverted into monopolistic arrangements for exploitation of other groups in society, to the extent that employers and unions "cooperate" in fixing prices, limiting entry of competitors into the business, and restricting output. In such cases, collective bar-

178

gaining and union-management cooperation have degenerated into collective collusion. If giant corporations are potentially dangerous as monopolies, they may be twice as dangerous in combination with giant unions. Monopolies that have as their primary objective the restriction of output are contrary to the public interest.

High on the list of management's bill of complaints against organized labor is the charge that unions seek to *standardize individual productivity at the average level that the group can attain*. In thus holding back the more energetic and ambitious individuals, it is management's claim that incentives are destroyed, and, consequently, working-force efficiency is undermined.

It is wrong to assume, however, that unions are solely responsible for restriction of output on the part of workers. Factual studies made by members of the Committee on Human Relations in Industry demonstrate very clearly that restriction of output in some form exists in nearly all establishments, on all sorts of jobs, under all kinds of payment systems, and *in unorganized as well as unionized plants*. Professor Burleigh Gardner has concluded that on nearly every job, workers have some understanding of a day's work that serves as a standard of performance for the group. He also points out that one of the most important factors impelling workers to limit output is a general suspicion that management is motivated by a desire to get more work out of them for the wages paid.

I would go further and state that employees tend to limit output for fear of working themselves out of a job. American workers have a conviction, gained through experience, that the number of jobs is limited and that, except for brief periods of time such as a war emergency, there are not enough jobs to go around. Because they have been out of work or have seen others suffer unemployment in business depressions, they lack confidence in the ability of American enterprise to assure adequate employment. A very large segment of our working population is motivated by a "job-scarcity consciousness," and it is this attitude on the part of workers that explains why unions are often compelled to insist on restriction of output.

Even where management wholeheartedly accepts unions and unions unconditionally accept the functions of management, we still find that workers often restrict output either informally or by direct agreement. On the railroads, for example, we have all sorts of make-work or "featherbed" rules, yet union-management relations are cooperative and harmonious. We commonly think that union-employer relations in England are far more advanced than in this country, yet output restrictions are common in nearly all British plants. These conditions will continue to exist, in organized or unorganized plants, as long as the majority of workers fear unemployment. In theory, workers and unionists agree that undue restriction of output is uneconomic—that increased productivity is necessary to raise living standards. Yet, in practice, they will try to "make the work last longer" when jobs are scarce.

Obviously, the ability of individual companies to guarantee employment is limited. Few establishments in this country, for example, could guarantee full employment on an annual basis. Even the unions now pressing for the adoption of the "annual wage" recognize this. There is a growing recognition on the part of workers, unions, and many employers that government must assist in assuring full employment. For example, opinion polls show that, for a solution of the postwar job problem, twice as many workers look to the government as to company heads.

Call it what we wish, the "full employment" issue will have far-reaching influence on the future course of labor-management relations, and we are not going to solve the problem of restriction of output until we find a cure for the problem of unemployment. To the extent that labor unions appear to be pressing for programs for full employment while employers appear to be favoring a return to the good old days of the 1920's, union leaders will be thought of as progressives, while employers will be classed as reactionaries. This would widen the gulf between management and organized labor. Now that unions are stressing political action in addition to collective bargaining, the area of potential competition for the allegiance of job-conscious workers has become much wider. Consequently, effective labor-management cooperation at the plant level is likely to be influenced to an increasing extent by the type of collaboration labor and management achieve in political and national affairs. We have here a problem that transcends the boundaries of labor economics and human relations—a problem of how to make large-scale democracy work in a country where diverse functional as well as geographical interests must be harmonized.

Government must play an important role in providing unemployment insurance, a system of old-age annuities, old-age assistance, and financial protection of workers against injuries and sickness. There is a growing recognition by workers, unions, and many companies, also, that the government must take definite steps to assure high-level productive employment in a peacetime economy. On this score the economic interests of unions, employers, and employees are not in conflict, although there are some more or less ideological differences of opinion regarding the appropriate scope of government activity. These differences could be largely resolved by an objective and factual consideration by management and labor of the problems and issues involved.

It will be a calamity, however, if a comprehensive social security program and a national policy for assuring employment are supported by organized labor and opposed by organized management. If workers identify employers with reaction and unions with progressive measures, it may be

almost impossible to develop cooperative human relationships at the plant level. A militant class-conscious labor
movement might then gain ground by preaching the doctrine
that "the only good employer is a dead one" and that social
justice can be achieved only by an overthrow of the system
of private enterprise.

Collaboration between nations is required to maintain a
lasting peace, and such collaboration requires give-and-take
—compromise, if you will—by national interests that are
often divergent. On the domestic scene, industrial peace
may depend upon similar collaboration and give-and-take by
management and organized labor. The vast majority of
companies and unions must reach agreement on a common
course of political action, thus isolating the small groups of
extremists in unions and die-hard reactionaries in industry
who would plunge this country into prolonged and bitter
industrial warfare.

Chapter X

INDUSTRY AND SOCIETY

MODERN American industry has performed miracles of production; and continuing advances in science and technology give promise of unlimited improvements in our standard of living—provided the problems of full employment and mass distribution of goods can be mastered. But as science and technology have advanced, the capacity of the industrial organization to elicit the cooperation of its members has undergone a serious deterioration.

The common understandings, the face-to-face contacts, which served in many cases to bind all the members together when the enterprises were small, have given way to large-scale, impersonal organizations in which communication moves predominantly in one direction—from the top down. Men at the bottom or even in intermediate levels tend to feel that management is out of touch with them and has no interest in the problems they face. When such a situation arises, the organization can no longer pull together as a team. Cooperation gives way to friction and friction leads to open conflict.

In recent years management has been undertaking to build up personnel departments and related activities in order to cope with this problem. While much sound work has been done along these lines, the effort has been handicapped by certain common misconceptions that have prevented management from conceiving the problem in terms that will permit a practical solution.

The personnel man and the executive have been misled by the individualistic point of view, which is so popular in our society. With this approach, organizational and human relations problems become problems of individuals and of individual skills, aptitudes, and personalities.

If there is friction among individuals, it is blamed upon their personality traits. Joe is too aggressive; Tom is sullen and uncooperative, and so on. Of course, we grant that individuals differ widely from one another and that these individual differences must be taken into account in any effort to understand an organization. However, whenever we attempt to apply the individualistic point of view to the pressing problems of the day, we are forced to recognize its shortcomings. If one foreman is emotionally upset, we may be able to explain his behavior in individual personality terms—at least in part. But if all or a large number of the foremen of a given company organize to bargain collectively with management, then clearly we cannot explain this by saying that the foremen are maladjusted personalities. Rather, it is the system of human relations in the organization that has become maladjusted, and readjustment can be achieved only through applying knowledge of human relations in industry.

The individualistic point of view has also led to an oversimplified conception of the worker's relationship to his job. "The right man in the right job" has been a powerful slogan for many years. While it is certainly important to place a man on a job that is in line with his interests and abilities, it does not follow that aptitude tests will prove effective guides to individual adjustment. The Western Electric researchers found no relationship between aptitude test scores and production records. Those tests were made two decades ago, and perhaps present-day tests are of more use, but even if they did sort out people according to the jobs they were best qualified to do, that would hardly solve the problem. The worker's adjustment to his job is determined only in part by his skill and aptitude. Our research shows that his attitude toward his job is determined in very large measure by his relations with fellow workers and with his foreman. If he fits in with the gang and gets along with the boss, he is inclined to be satisfied with his job. If he doesn't get along with fellow workers or foreman, then he doesn't like the job. These are problems in human relations.

Management has also been handicapped by acceptance of an oversimplified theory of human motivation. It has been commonly assumed that the working man is motivated primarily, if not exclusively, by a desire for material rewards. Therefore, if a man is offered good wages and reasonable economic security, he should be satisfied. When he is not, his discontent is often blamed upon "outside agitators."

The Western Electric research, along with innumerable studies of primitive and civilized societies, has shown that human motivation is an exceedingly complex thing, with economic rewards being only one factor.

While economic incentives are still given primary emphasis in industry, their limitations are coming to be more recognized. However, in many cases this has led management off in vain pursuit of some other simple factors that will solve the problem. Industry has gone in for insurance plans, employee recreation, plant libraries, recorded music, free vitamin pills, inspirational posters, and various other supposed morale builders. Some of these efforts have met with favorable reactions, but none of them touch the heart of the problem: the relations of the individuals to one another in the social system.

This discussion of management attitudes is, of course, an overstatement of the case. There are many skillful executives, supervisors, and personnel men, who do not think and act in the oversimplified categories presented here. They recognize that they are dealing with a social system, and they govern their behavior accordingly. However, in most cases this recognition is a matter of intuition and unorganized common sense. The executive does not have the systematic, scientific knowledge that may be at his command in regard to other subjects, such as physics, chemistry, and engineering.

This lack arises in the first instance from the backward state of the science of human relations. Compared with the natural and physical sciences, knowledge in this field is still in a very primitive state. However, over the past several decades, important advances have been made. While this is only a beginning, the knowledge already available in this science can provide the executive, personnel man, or union official with valuable tools for understanding and for skillful action.

This is not the place for a systematic statement of this body of knowledge. However, *Industry and Society* should serve to introduce some of the chief conclusions that have come out of research in this field.

In the first place, we must learn to look upon industry as a social system, a system of human relations, which regulates the behavior of the individual members. The behavior of the members will vary according to their individual personalities, to be sure, but it will be importantly influenced by the *place* each individual occupies in the system of human relations. We find that people occupying the same place in this system tend to have similar attitudes and reactions toward other people. Therefore it is not possible to think constructively or act skillfully concerning the problems of individuals in the organization unless the nature of the social system is first explored and analyzed.

Our analysis in this volume has centered upon three key ideas that may be stated briefly but will then require some elaboration.

1. The factory is, in one respect, a status system, and this

system is closely related to the status system of the community. The two systems are mutually interdependent so that changes in one inevitably have an impact upon the other.

2. The factory has a formal organization (as everyone recognizes) and also an informal organization. The factory cannot operate harmoniously unless these two types of structure are adjusted to each other.

3. The social system of the factory exists in a *state of equilibrium* when a customary pattern of status and human relations has been built up over a period of time. When changes are introduced, the system tends to react so as to reestablish its equilibrium. When sudden and drastic changes destroy this equilibrium, the members react with feelings of anxiety or aggression, loyalty to the organization is undermined, and effective cooperation breaks down.

Each of these points will be taken up and discussed in terms of the data presented in this volume.

When we talk of status, we must recognize that industry cannot be divorced from the society of which it is a part. The individual has status in his community and also at his place of work, and his behavior cannot be understood without a consideration of his position in both areas of his life.

This is clearly demonstrated in Warner's study of the strike in the Yankee City shoe factories. There it was found that the factory system had changed over a period of years and consequently had destroyed the orderly progression in status that the worker had enjoyed as he moved up step by step to more highly skilled jobs and gained for himself the accompanying status recognition in the community. The advance of technology, destroying status distinctions among workers, made possible for the first time the growth of union organization. The course of the strike was also influenced by changes in status among the managerial personnel. The local leaders of industry were no longer the top people of Yankee City society, and, in fact, some of those social leaders gave their support to the strike. Since control of the factories had passed out of the community, it became possible to symbolize the union efforts as a strike against outside, enemy forces. This drama, so important to industry, was acted out not in the factory alone but in the total community.

These changes in status in factory and community have given rise to labor unions as organs of conflict with management, but, as Starr points out, the organization of conflict is by no means their only function. The changes described by Warner have upset the old social order based upon close personal relations between social classes with leadership and social responsibility resting in the hands of those of high status. As the old social equilibrium is destroyed, the workers need to reorient themselves to a new system of human relations. This reorientation takes place, not only in the factory, but also in their relations outside the factory. It involves readjustments in their total participation in community life. Unions have stepped in to function in this area also.

Just as the top executives of industry have been losing their power to act as spokesmen representing the workers of their factories, we find them also losing their leadership of the working class in the life of the community. As Starr points out, organized labor has been playing a steadily expanding role in furnishing leadership in social welfare and civic activities. The figures he gives are evidence of very fundamental changes that have been taking place in our American society. These changes do not point to an inevitable class struggle, but they do suggest that, for harmony in the community as well as in the plant, the social and business leaders must learn to deal with workers through the leadership arising in worker organizations themselves.

The old social equilibrium was based upon personal ties of workers, supervisors, and executives and also upon the opportunity of the individual to rise from the lowest status to reach a high place in plant and community. The changes outlined by Warner have very largely blocked off this route to mobility and split the workers from management. The developing new equilibrium substitutes for mobility and ties with "the higher ups" the sort of satisfactions that grow out of stabilizing and protecting the status of workers as a group under the leadership that grows out of worker organizations.

Status in the community is also important for an understanding of the motivation of workers in industry. As Davis points out, the goals sought by the individual are not born in him but are learned in the course of his social experience. Since individuals of different status are subject to different sorts of conditioning, it is natural for them to seek different satisfactions at work and in the community. As the conscientious worker has learned his good work habits, so has the erratic and undependable worker learned from his own social experience.

Davis shows that workers are not all alike—a point that is readily understood by management. But management tends to look upon worker differences as differences in personality, whereas Davis shows that differences in status are extremely important in the behavior of workers. The workers he discusses do not respond to the same rewards and punishments that are effective upon the more stable group of employees. Management can do a more effective job through recognizing these differences in status and motivation than is possible when it is assumed that all workers have (or should have) the goals in life that are cherished by management. Here again we have a problem that cannot be defined in terms of individual personalities, if management is to act with skill in building morale.

For management there is, of course, no easy answer to this problem, for, as Davis points out, stable work habits depend upon stable employment, and this bottom working-class group is always the first to drop out of jobs in times of depression. This then is not industry's problem alone. It is a matter of concern for our whole American society.

The importance of social status in work behavior is again illustrated in Whyte's discussion of the problems of the waitress. There we see that some of her difficulties arise from the inferior position she holds in relation to customers and, consequently, from the attitude they hold toward her.

While constructive thinking on human relations in industry must begin by giving attention to the status held by the people in question, we should not conceive status in static terms. In a society such as ours, people do not necessarily remain in the same positions all their lives. There are always large numbers of people moving up in the world—and also people dropping down. The socially mobile individual has different attitudes and acts in different ways from the stable individual of the same status. Whyte's study of waitress behavior indicates that even her nervous reactions vary according to whether she is stable or moving up or down in the social world.

When we turn from the community to industry itself, we find that business organizations have their own highly developed status systems. As Barnard points out, all executives have some intuitive familiarity with status in their organizations, but few of them conceive of it as being systematically organized. They tend to think of the organization in terms of the abilities and personal attributes of its members, sometimes regarding status as an extraneous factor that should be disregarded if possible. At the other extreme we find people who would prefer not to recognize status distinctions because they upset notions of social equality.

Barnard shows that status in formal organizations is neither an extraneous factor nor a parasitic growth of the ambitions of scheming individuals. Instead, it has important functions both for the individuals and for the organization itself.

The status system grows out of differences in abilities of individuals and differences in the difficulties and importance of various kinds of work. Formal status also serves to identify people in a convenient manner so that others know how to behave toward them. It further protects the individual from excessive claims made upon him and serves to give him a feeling of security in the organization.

A well-defined status system is indispensable to an efficient organization. It organizes the system of communication, and it facilitates the carrying out of orders. It offers incentives of prestige as well as monetary reward for superior performance. It also fixes responsibility and tends to develop a sense of responsibility in the individual.

On the other hand, as the system of positions becomes fixed, the organization labors under serious disadvantages. High status comes to be taken, of itself, as sufficient evidence of superior ability, so that it becomes difficult to evaluate the performance of the individual. As people develop vested interests in their positions, advancement on the basis of ability is undermined, and the organization loses the adaptability necessary to meet changing conditions.

On the one hand, the executive must recognize the importance of status and, at the same time, he must undertake to keep the system under control so that it will not destroy the effectiveness of the organization. Barnard provides no easy solution to this dilemma. Complex problems of human relations are not solved by neat formulas. But neither are they solved through attempting to ignore the existence of the status system. In fact, many serious morale problems arise through management's failure to recognize the nature of this system. An organization cannot operate effectively in terms of ability, aptitudes, and personality characteristics alone. It is a system of human relations in which the individual acts in terms of the status of himself and of other

191

members of the system. For effective action, therefore, the status system of the factory must be understood.

The factory structure should also be looked at in terms of its formal and informal organization. The formal organization requires little comment, for it is well recognized, and its importance is generally overemphasized. While it is quite true that a factory could not function without its formal line of authority and allocation of duties, it is also true that the factory could not operate on this basis alone. As Gardner points out, teamwork in industry depends upon the building up of a body of informal relationships, so that the business organization is made up of a number of cliques or friendship groups. These cannot be done away with without serious damage to the organization, even when they arise out of resistance to management activities. It is the task of the skillful executive or supervisor to help new people find their way into some social group and then to tie all the cliques together so that they function as part of a team instead of as competing or conflicting units.

The adjustment of human relations in industry cannot be accomplished through the formal organization, through the giving of orders and the writing of reports. As Hughes points out, the successful adjustment of the various races in industry can be achieved only by working through the informal organization. It is only in this area that it is possible to manipulate the mental and emotional processes of people so as to build a harmonious organization. And this is true not only of race relations but of human relations generally throughout the system. The successful executive therefore cannot rely simply upon his "power" to get orders carried out. To carry his organization along with him, he also needs understanding, skill, and personal influence.

The Western Electric research demonstrated the importance of the informal organization in the actual processes of production. A more recent study by Elton Mayo and

George F. F. Lombard showed the close relationship between a cohesive informal organization and a low rate of labor turnover and absenteeism. In the present volume, Whyte shows that the nervous tensions in the work situation can only be kept in balance if the worker has a secure place in the informal organization of his shop.

These conclusions apply not only to workers. They are equally applicable to the top levels of the organization. As Barnard points out, the effectiveness of top management depends upon its members being able to respond to each other in the habitual patterns that arise out of close association. Coordination cannot be achieved simply through the issuing of orders and the writing of memorandums. It arises out of a constantly recurring pattern of human relations through which the individual learns what to expect from others and how to react to others.

We have seen that industry involves a status system and a formal and informal organization of human relations. We have also seen an advancing technology and a changing society imposing changes upon industry, and we have seen these changes meeting resistance from within the structure.

Management may look upon such resistances to change simply as obstructions in the path of progress, which should be swept brusquely aside. This is an exceedingly costly approach to the problem. Management may be able to make fairly close estimates of the dollars and cents costs in materials and labor used to install the new plan, but there will always and inevitably be costs or savings in the field of human relations that accompany such changes. They cannot be so closely estimated, but management can act with more intelligence and skill if these factors are taken into consideration.

Gardner writes that any changes that threaten to lower the status or prestige of the group and of the individual, reduce the authority and scope of action and decision, or

193

disrupt habitual routines may be expected to give rise to resistance from individuals and groups of workers. Human relations run most smoothly when it is possible to build up unchanging patterns. However, it is obvious that a society such as ours cannot remain static. Changes necessarily take place and cannot be ignored. The skillful executive will not seek simply to avoid change but will explore the human as well as the technical elements involved in the change and take steps to compensate for the social disturbances that may result.

The problem may be conceived in terms of maintaining a state of equilibrium, similar to that observed in the natural sciences. When this equilibrium is upset, individuals and groups become disturbed and undertake to reestablish the old pattern or to work out some new adjustment. To function efficiently, the organization must develop some sort of fairly stable equilibrium. This may mean that changes are constantly being introduced into the system, but that they proceed slowly and that people are given time and help in adjusting themselves to new relationships.

The problem of low morale among foremen can best be understood in terms of disturbed equilibrium and of efforts to reach a new equilibrium through developing new relationships with management. In mass production industries, the foreman has found himself in an increasingly difficult position. Rapid technological developments have forced him to adjust and readjust to changes in patterns of work. The growth of personnel, cost control, engineering, and research departments has steadily restricted the authority and freedom of action of the first line supervisor. Finally, the growth of labor unions has given workers the right of appeal over the foreman's head and the chance to challenge his leadership. If the foreman feels pushed by management, he can no longer work his problem out in a unionized shop through simply pushing his workers; and the union, report-

194

ing on his behavior upstairs, can place him in a very insecure position.

The foreman might be able to work out his problems within the traditional framework, if he felt free to communicate with his superiors and to initiate action for them. However, placed at the next to bottom level of a monumental pyramid of authority, he feels that there is no chance of effective upward communication in the existing structure; and therefore he turns to organizations such as the Foreman's Association of America to speak and act for him. In other words, he builds up a new set of relationships to re-establish the equilibrium he lost through the changes outlined above.

The growth of union organization can be explained through the same scheme. First it should be noted that unions, like other segments of the factory organization, cannot be understood simply in terms of the factory structure itself. As Warner points out through his case study of the Yankee City strike, unions tend to gain impetus through certain changes that are and have been taking place in American society. Along with this development, as Starr shows, the unions have been playing an expanding role in the life of the community.

While it is impossible to generalize for all workers, we may say in general that the worker wants security in his job. That does not mean that he is not interested in advancement. It does mean that he wants to know from day to day, week to week, and year to year, where he stands and what he can expect from his employment. As he fits into the factory structure, he also develops relationships with fellow workers, which make an important contribution to his social life. In other words, he finds a place in the informal organization that is very essential to the morale of the company and to the well-being of the workers.

Now, top management may make decisions that disrupt

the informal organization of workers, lower the status of many individuals, and destroy the worker's sense of security. Especially in large organizations with many levels of authority, unorganized workers cannot effectively protest such action. Given the difficulty of communicating from the bottom up, they cannot make their complaints heard and understood at the top level.

We need not assume that top management acts with malice or is indifferent to the interests of the workers. In some cases we have studied, the disturbances resulted from action that was intended to benefit the workers. Unfortunately management had too narrow a conception of worker interests. Decisions were based upon the logics of economics and technology, and no consideration was given to the requirements of the system for maintaining its state of social equilibrium. Union organization functions, in part, to build up a new equilibrium through establishing communication with top management and through resisting decisions that would upset relationships at the work level.

We should not think, however, that the new equilibrium is reached as soon as the union is successful in organizing the workers. As Gardner and Harbison point out, the beginning stages of a collective bargaining relationship require all sorts of difficult adjustments within the management and union structures as well as between management and union. To achieve such adjustments requires time, imagination, and skill for the leaders on both sides. Before a really harmonious relationship can develop, according to Harbison's argument, it is necessary for both sides to work out new areas of cooperation so that union and management are convinced that the other party to the contract is making a constructive contribution.

The instances of such union-management collaboration are as yet far fewer than those where friction and conflict prevail; but, if industry were prepared to devote a fraction of the time, effort, study, and financing now expended in technological research to research in human relations, it might yet be possible to establish an enduring peace upon our industrial battle front.

This volume has presented a point of view, a new approach to the human problems of industry. The bibliography that follows will provide further background material for the understanding of industry as a social system and will also give references upon the working out of certain specific problems in human relations. However, in no sense should *Industry and Society* and the accompanying references be considered a comprehensive treatment of this field.

Research workers have only just begun this exploration. There is far more to be learned than has yet been discovered. And the learning process requires not only research but active experimentation in industry so that the conclusions of research may be tested in practice. The Committee on Human Relations in Industry of The University of Chicago, with the collaboration of industrial concerns and labor unions, is now carrying on a steadily expanding program involving both research and experimentation. As the results come in, they will be published in this *Human Relations in Industry Series*.

The great discoveries of the natural sciences, culminating in the use of atomic energy, have placed in man's hands unlimited power to destroy his own civilization. The scientists who have played a leading role in this world-shattering research are appalled at the power—for good or evil—that they have unleashed. Humanitarians cry out to all nations to renounce the use of the atomic bomb for all future times, and yet it should be obvious that such promises are valueless unless the underlying conflicts among peoples are first worked out. The fruits of the natural sciences can neither be outlawed nor forgotten. Whether they destroy us or usher in a better life depends also upon science—the science of human relations. Immature though it is, this science already offers to man some of the tools he needs for his very life, and the urgency of the hour impels us all to make every effort to improve the tools we have and to discover the tools we need for the adjustment of the conflicts that are rending the fabric of our society.

ABOUT THE AUTHORS

Industry and Society grew out of a Human Relations in Industry lecture series given at The University of Chicago in the summer of 1945. The eight lectures were delivered by Chester I. Barnard, Mark Starr, and the six faculty members of the Committee on Human Relations in Industry who are represented in this volume. The first and last chapters are the exclusive responsibility of the faculty participants.

CHESTER I. BARNARD

Chester I. Barnard has been president of the New Jersey Bell Telephone Company since 1927. He has also served in many capacities in government and social service. He organized the Emergency Relief Administration of the state of New Jersey and was its director from 1931 to 1933 and again during most of 1935. In 1941 he served as assistant to the Secretary of the Treasury. From 1942 to 1945 he was president of the United Service Organizations, Inc. (USO), rendering recreational and other services to the personnel of our armed forces throughout the world. He is the author of *The Functions of the Executive* and has lectured frequently at Harvard and Princeton Universities on organization, administration, and social-science subjects.

ALLISON DAVIS

Allison Davis is a member of the Department of Education, The University of Chicago, having been trained in social anthropology. He is coauthor of *Children of Bondage*, a study of the development of Negro adolescent personality, and of *Deep South*, a study of the social organization of a southern city. He is now conducting a large-scale project on intelligence testing for the purpose of constructing tests that will

199

be more practical than those in current use for industrial and business personnel offices.

Burleigh B. Gardner

Burleigh B. Gardner is assistant professor of industrial relations, School of Business, and executive secretary of the Committee on Human Relations in Industry of The University of Chicago. Trained in social anthropology, he did his first fieldwork in a study of Negro-white relations in a southern city. For five years he was in charge of the employee relations research section, Hawthorne plant, Western Electric Company, where he was active in the development of the company's well-known personnel counseling program. He is author of the recently published *Human Relations in Industry* and co-author of *Deep South*.

Frederick H. Harbison

Frederick H. Harbison is a member of the Department of Economics and the executive officer of the Industrial Relations Center of The University of Chicago. A specialist in the field of labor relations, he served the government during the war as Labor and Manpower Counselor, Petroleum Administrator for War, and also as consultant to the War Production Board, the Army Service Forces, and the War Manpower Commission.

The volume, *How Collective Bargaining Works*, contains his study of union-management relations in the steel industry. He is also the author of *Seniority Policies and Procedures as Developed through Collective Bargaining* and of *Seniority Problems during Demobilization and Reconversion*.

Everett C. Hughes

Everett C. Hughes is a member of the Department of Sociology of The University of Chicago and is director of the race relations in industry study of the Committee on Human Relations in Industry. He has studied racial and ethnic relations in Germany, eastern Canada, and the United States.

His *French Canada in Transition* is a study of the relations of French and English in the social and economic structure of a growing industrial community in Quebec. His chapter in *Industry and Society* discusses some of the findings of the in-plant and community studies carried on by Negro and white research assistants on his staff.

J. O. Low

J. O. Low was a member of W. Lloyd Warner's Yankee City research staff. With Warner, he is coauthor of Volume IV in the Yankee City Series, *The Social System of the Modern Factory*.

Mark Starr

Mark Starr is educational director of the International Ladies' Garment Workers' Union. Born in Great Britain, he began work in the mines of South Wales. He came to this country to teach British labor history at Brookwood Labor College and also taught in the Bryn Mawr Summer School. He has been president of Local 189, American Federation of Teachers, and a national vice-president of that union.

He is author of *A Worker Looks at History, Trade Unionism: Past and Future, A Worker Looks at Economics, Lies and Hate in Education*, and is coauthor of *Workers' Education in the United States* and *Labor in America*, a fourth-year high-school textbook.

W. Lloyd Warner

W. Lloyd Warner is a member of the Departments of Anthropology and Sociology and chairman of the Committee on Human Relations in Industry of The University of Chicago. He is also a member of the Committee on Human Development. Beginning his research with a three-year study of Australian aborigines (*A Black Civilization*), he returned to this country to apply the field methods and approach of the social anthropologists to modern, civilized communities. The leading figure in this development, he directed a study of a New England community while a member of the Department of Anthropology at Harvard University and of the Department of Industrial Research, Harvard School of Business Administration.

INDUSTRY AND SOCIETY

Three volumes of the Yankee City Series have appeared, and two more are in preparation.

While at Chicago, he has conducted studies of the Chicago Negro community (*Color and Human Nature*) and of education and social stratification (*Who Shall Be Educated?*). He is currently directing research in human development and social organization in a Middle Western town.

WILLIAM FOOTE WHYTE

William Foote Whyte is an associate professor of Sociology of The University of Chicago. His chapter grows out of research financed and sponsored by the National Restaurant Association. Previously he carried on research on human relations in the petroleum industry. His first research project was a three and a half year study of corner gangs and political and racket organizations of a metropolitan slum district. This led to the publication of *Street Corner Society*.

Some of The University of Chicago research reported in this volume was made possible by the support of the following organizations: Container Corporation of America; Goodman Manufacturing Company; Libby, McNeill and Libby; Sears, Roebuck & Company; Soreng Manufacturing Company; Visking Corporation; Western Shade Cloth Company, and the National Restaurant Association.

WORKING BIBLIOGRAPHY

It is not our intention to present a comprehensive bibliography covering all the available literature related to this book. We feel that it will be more useful to present a selected list of titles together with comments on each one so that readers will know what to expect from the various references.

Those interested in the scheme of analysis of *Industry and Society* will find further material of value in the following references:

1. *The Factory as a Social System:*

BARNARD, CHESTER I.: *The Functions of the Executive,* Harvard University Press, Cambridge, 1939. An analysis of human relations in business and other formal organizations, with special reference to the role of the executive.

GARDNER, BURLEIGH B.: *Human Relations in Industry,* Richard D. Irwin, Inc., Chicago, 1945. Presents the approach of *Industry and Society* in a systematic way. The most valuable general volume for an understanding of human relations in industry.

ROETHLISBERGER, F. J.: *Management and Morale.* Harvard University Press, Cambridge, 1943. Presents in brief form the conclusions drawn from the Western Electric research.

——— and W. J. DICKSON: *Management and the Worker,* Harvard University Press, Cambridge, 1939. A full report on the Western Electric research and experimental program.

WARNER, W. L., and J. O. LOW: *The Social System of the Modern Factory,* Yale University Press, New Haven, to be published in 1946. A study of the social organization of the modern factory in a New England city.

2. *Status and the Community:*

DAVIS, ALLISON, and BURLEIGH B. and MARY R. GARDNER: *Deep South,* The University of Chicago Press, Chicago, 1941. A study of the social structure and of race relations in a southern city.

HUGHES, EVERETT C.: *French Canada in Transition,* The University of Chicago Press, Chicago, 1943. A study of the relations of French and English in the social structure of a French-Canadian city. Discusses the place of each group in the industrial organization.

WARNER, W. LLOYD, and Associates: *Yankee City Series,* Yale University Press, New Haven. Volumes so far published are *The Social Life of a Modern Community,* 1941, *The Status System of a Modern Community,* 1942, and *The Social Systems of American Ethnic Groups,* 1945. *The Social System of the Modern Factory* will be published in 1946. These volumes report on a comprehensive and intensive study of the social organization and social life of a small New England industrial city. Casual readers will find that the introductory "profile" sections of these books give the "feel" of the social structure of the city and aid them in recognizing status in everyday life. Volume IV will be especially valuable for those interested in the relationship between industry and society.

3. *Informal Organization:*

MAYO, ELTON, and GEORGE F. F. LOMBARD: *Teamwork and Labor Turnover in the Aircraft Industry of Southern California,* publication of the Harvard Graduate School of Business Administration, Boston, 1944. This study shows the importance of informal organization in reducing labor turnover.

ROETHLISBERGER, F. J., and W. J. DICKSON: *Management and the Worker,* Harvard University Press, Cambridge, 1939. Part IV, pp. 379-548, presents the best case studies of informal work groups that have yet appeared.

WHYTE, WILLIAM F.: *Street Corner Society*, The University of Chicago Press, Chicago, 1943. An analysis of the role of the informal group in an urban, working-class district. This type of analysis is readily adaptable to the understanding of informal organization in industry.

4. *Problems of Supervisors and of Supervision:*

GARDNER, BURLEIGH B., and WILLIAM F. WHYTE: *The Man in the Middle: Position and Problems of the Foreman.* Published as a special issue of *Applied Anthropology Magazine*, Spring, 1945. Available from the Society for Applied Anthropology, 10 Frisbie Place, Cambridge, Mass. An analysis of the problems faced by the foreman in his relations with subordinates and superiors.

ROETHLISBERGER, F. J.: "The Foreman: Master and Victim of Double Talk," *Harvard Business Review*, Spring, 1945. An analysis of the problems of the foreman in relation to top management and to staff organizations.

WHYTE, WILLIAM F.: *Human Problems of the Restaurant Industry*, McGraw-Hill Book Company, Inc., New York, to be published in 1947. Part IV, "Human Elements in Supervision," discusses the type of organization of human relations that is necessary for building cooperation. While the material is drawn from the restaurant industry, the conclusions apply to industry in general.

5. *Race Relations in Industry:*

FELDMAN, HERMAN: *Racial Factors in American Industry*, Harper & Brothers, New York, 1931. General report of a large-scale study. Sections on various immigrant groups as well as on the Negro.

GARDNER, BURLEIGH B.: *Human Relations in Industry*, Chap. XI, "Minority Groups in Industry," Richard D. Irwin, Inc., Chicago, 1945. A general book with one chapter that applies the point of view of the present volume to the problems of race in industry.

205

HUGHES, EVERETT C.: *French-Canada in Transition*, Chap. VII, "French and English in the Industrial Hierarchy," The University of Chicago Press, Chicago, 1943. A case study of the relations between ethnic groups in an industrial community.

JOHNSON, CHARLES S.: *Patterns of Negro Segregation*, Harper & Brothers, New York, 1944. Most recent general and authoritative work on the Negro and labor unions.

SHIH KUO-HENG: *China Enters the Machine Age*, Harvard University Press, Cambridge, 1944. A case study of the industrialization of a peasant people.

STERNER, RICHARD: *The Negro's Share*, Harper & Brothers, New York, 1943. Comprehensive study of the place of the Negro in the economy of the United States.

WARNER, W. LLOYD, and LEO SROLE: *The Social Systems of American Ethnic Groups*, Yale University Press, New Haven, 1945. Chapter IV, "The Ethnic Groups in the Economic Life of the Community," presents a systematic analysis of the occupational roles of various ethnic groups in a typical New England manufacturing town. Especially valuable because the economic data are put into the setting of the whole social life of the community.

6. *Union Organization:*

GARDNER, BURLEIGH B.: *Human Relations in Industry*, Richard D. Irwin, Inc., Chicago, 1945. Chapter V, "The Union: Its Functions and Place in the Structure," shows how the union operates in relation to the factory structure.

GOLDEN, CLINTON S., and HAROLD RUTTENBERG: *Dynamics of Industrial Democracy*, Harper & Brothers, New York, 1942. Discusses the place and functions of unions in industry and society from the point of view of organized labor (CIO).

MILLIS, HARRY A., and ROYAL E. MONTGOMERY: *Organized Labor*, McGraw-Hill Book Company, Inc., New York, 1945. A thorough statement and analysis of the structure, functions, and policies of labor unions.

SELEKMAN, BENJAMIN M.: "When the Union Enters," and "Administering the Union Agreement," *Harvard Business Review*, Winter and Spring, 1945. Analyzes the human relations adjustments to be made in building up a new relationship between union and management.

SLICHTER, SUMNER H.: *Union Policies and Industrial Management*, Brookings Institution, Washington, D. C., 1941. A study of different types of union-management relations.

WHYTE, WILLIAM F.: "Who Goes Union and Why?" *Personnel Journal*, December, 1944. Analyzes the varying reactions of workers to a union organization drive in terms of the equilibrium theory of interaction presented in the present volume.

INDEX

209